D0996569

The Poems of Catullus

THE POEMS OF CATULLUS

Translated by
Frederic Raphael and
Kenneth McLeish

JONATHAN CAPE
THIRTY BEDFORD SQUARE LONDON

First published 1978
© 1978 by Volatic Ltd and Kenneth McLeish

Jonathan Cape Limited
30 Bedford Square, London WC1

British Library Cataloguing in Publication Data
Catullus, Gaius Valerius
The poems of Catullus.
I. Raphael, Frederic   II. McLeish, Kenneth
874'.01   PA6275.E5
ISBN 0-224-01599-0

CENTRAL |
GLASS
NO.   874
             CAT
CAT
BBC LIBRARY

Printed in Great Britain by The Anchor Press Ltd
and bound by Wm Brendon & Son Ltd
both of Tiptree, Essex.

for Michael Ayrton

Contents

Introduction

Tennyson called him tender; Harold Nicolson was
unable to understand why. Gaius Valerius Catullus, the
greatest Roman lyric poet, who was said by St Jerome to
have died at the age of thirty, has always excited
contradictory judgments. He is prized by some for the
sincerity and deprecated by others for the crudeness of
his feelings; romantics credit him with spontaneity,
classics with erudition; his eroticism gives him a
dubious reputation among the austere; the sentimental
see in his delicacy the very instance of the sensibility
which proves too fine for this world: those whom the
Muses love, they say, die young.

Of the specific nature of his death nothing is known,
and of his life very little. Did the cruelties of his mistress
indeed bring on despair and death? He may as well have
died of malaria or in a street accident. (Juvenal, a
century and a half later, reminds us that such things
were commonplace.) Perhaps like Cinna, his friend and
the unluckiest of poets, he was killed in some brawl
which did not concern him personally - or, like
Marlowe, in one that concerned him closely, for
Catullus had a savage tongue as well as a tender heart.
He was reckless enough, and brave enough, to make
savage fun of Caesar and of Pompey (poems 29, 54, 57,
etc.) at a time when a dagger in the back was a more
likely response to libel than a civilised injunction. We
are promised that Caesar took the young man's ribaldry
in good part, but Catullus hit with contemptuous
accuracy right below the belt, his favourite target. He
saw the republic collapsing into tyranny and in that

collapse of public modesty he read the ruin of his own hopes of a decent life among decent people, and he raged accordingly. Rome had never been a just society in any egalitarian sense, but it had been governed according to conventions of self-restraint (the consuls yielding power annually to their elected successors) and respect for the common good, however narrowly that might be interpreted. The vanity of wealth and the megalomania of conquest were in the process of rupturing all that, and forever. But though he was a caustic observer of social degeneration, it would be quite false to represent Catullus as a revolutionary; like many young aristocrats when they devote themselves to the arts, he was more disgusted by the graceless style of *ces princes qui nous gouvernent* than the advocate of any ideology of social change. He was a sort of Tory romantic (if one must plump for an anachronism): like so many ancient poets, he affected to revere the values of the golden age, whenever that was. In an age of shifting political and sexual alliances, he dreamed of fidelity and true friendship. His denunciations of his mistress, pitched at the highest level of poetic despair, and even of the dinner guest who stole his napkins, pitched somewhat lower, might prove tiresome in their whining reproach, were it not that one has a sense always of a dream of true constancy and affection muffled by the sour blanket of reality. 'It need not be like this' is ever at war with 'this is how it is'. Such tension is at the heart of the Catullan character; hate and love rise and fall on an eternal see-saw, each counter-weighted and held in suspense by the other.

Catullus was probably born about 84 B.C., if we are to accept Jerome's statement that he died at thirty, since poem 29 alludes to Caesar's conquest of Britain, which took place in 55 B.C. (Jerome says that he was born in 87 B.C., but this is incompatible with the text.) But the

10

date of his death is of merely academic interest, for his immortality is assured. His best poems speak with a directness unique in surviving Roman literature. One need not disparage Horace and Virgil, Lucretius and Ovid, or indeed Propertius and Juvenal, to justify the view that Catullus is a case gloriously apart. It was not always so. His work disappeared from public knowledge for the best part of a thousand years and he might easily have shared the fate of Cinna, who not only perished in the flesh because he happened to be mistaken for a hated politician of the same name, but whose poems also failed to elude the *oubliette* of time: scarcely a line remains. Catullus himself survives only because some wine merchant in his native city of Verona chose, in the fourteenth century, to stuff a bundle of his poems in an unused measuring vessel. (The story that they were wedged in a wine cask is a romance.) From that precarious source - the so-called Veronensis MS - all our present manuscripts derive.

What proportion of the poet's complete output the existing 113 poems represent, no one can say. There are fragments and traces of poems which are not represented in the present *œuvre*. Some scholars believe that these are the selected works as collated and edited by Catullus himself; others maintain that they cannot be regarded as definitive. Equally, one party declares that it is absurd to suppose that the poet himself arranged them in so haphazard, even silly, an order; the other insists that there is subtle art in the apparently casual interleaving of passion with pretentiousness, of satire with sentiment. Professor J. P. Sullivan has kindly pointed out that Professor Clausen strongly believes that no ancient editor would have classified a poetic corpus by *metre*. No doubt Catullus did indeed issue a *libellus*, but the present text, in both Clausen's and Sullivan's view, is the work of a later editor. This does not, of course, mean that no signs are evident of the poet's own adroit juxtapositions. Certainly Catullus was a master of *variatio*: his poems rang the changes on metre and subject in a manner which was indeed, in a literary sense, revolutionary. He drew his inspiration from the Greek poets of Alexandria, above all Callimachus who, in a famous and prescriptive polemic, pronounced the superiority of the contemporary short poem over the long. Catullus endorsed his view that a thoroughly elaborated small work was in every way better than a sprawling, jerry-built long one (see poems 22, 36 and 95). It used to be said that he deplored longer poems because he was incapable of writing them: one of the 'problems' of Catullus was that his *œuvre* was broken abruptly into two halves, the successful shorter works and the allegedly inferior longer ones, 61-68. This supposed dichotomy - the idea of 'two Catulluses' - does not endure sympathetic scrutiny, although it remains true that the long poems are longer than the short ones. The same poet is unmistakably at work in both areas and the same obsessions reveal themselves. It has been suggested that poem 63, for instance, was written as a kind of exercise, because Catullus was concerned to discover whether or not he could handle the metrical difficulties. If it is true that every conscious artist (and Catullus was certainly that) is likely to present himself with stylistic challenges, like a great golfer who disdains the easy shot as unworthy of his idea of himself, the terrible *donnée* of poem 63, the castration theme, has surely a more than academic significance. Catullus' sense of being somehow irrevocably unmanned by his, as they say, ball-crushing mistress gives the Attis poem a characteristic personality. Some scholars have suggested that it is merely a translation from Callimachus, though no Callimachan poem on the theme is known to us. Here again we may say that, even if such a poem existed, Catullus chose this particular one and made it his own, just as the 'Imitations' of Robert Lowell are very much Lowell. An inspired translator does not translate just anything.

The old debating points recur frequently in one's attempts to understand Catullus. Did he write for others or for himself? Did he rely on inspiration or was he hardly more than a gifted *pasticheur*? Was he serious or was he flippant, a unique genius or merely the sole instance to come down to us of a whole school of similar talents? If his generation did indeed boast of several poets of his quality, it must have been uniquely blessed, for its sky blazed with suns. Yet Catullus certainly did belong to a movement, famously labelled by Cicero 'the *neoteroi*', which could mean merely 'the newer/younger ones', though one suspects a sarcastic overtone to the soubriquet. Cicero larded his letters with Greek tags and was an honest admirer of Greek culture, but the Hellenistic affectations of those brilliant young men who looked to Alexandria for their models probably struck him as both suspect and impertinent. The iconoclastic wit of men like Cinna, Calvus (another possible genius lost to us forever) and Catullus gave them, it seemed, an easy *entrée* into the highest social circles, where their affectations of disdain for the prosaic platitudes of public life must have added to Cicero's sense of uneasiness. There was, he might be forgiven for thinking, something positively dangerous about a drop-out who could drop in on the smartest people and take his place among them with only an arrogant epigram to serve as a calling card. Cicero himself was regarded by Catullus with ambivalence: witness the two ways of reading poem 49. A man capable of celebrating his consulship and the victory over Catiline with a verse like *O fortunatam natam me consule Romam* (lucky Rome, born again with me as consul) can scarcely have been regarded with undiluted admiration by a poet who placed a premium on subtlety. The *neoteroi* formed an aristocracy of taste, with a slang and style of its own, and Cicero - himself a 'new man' socially and politically - must have felt his exclusion with something of the bitterness of one who, having travelled hopefully, liked to think that he had now undoubtedly arrived. That Catullus was soon in love with one of the sisters of Cicero's most implacable enemy salted the wound stingingly. However, it would be wrong to make too much of the antagonism between the Ciceronian and the Catullan view of life and of letters. If Cicero, who had so needed patrons when he began his career, was disposed, in middle age, to patronise the next generation, he recognised Catullus' quality with the grudging condescension of old talent for young genius.

Catullus may have paraded a certain patrician stylishness, but he was hardly less provincial in origin than Cicero himself. He came from Verona, where his father was a landowner sufficiently prominent to entertain Julius Caesar when the great man came through Cisalpine Gaul on official business. Catullus grew up on his father's estates by Lake Garda. As poem 31 proves, he remained devoted to the beauties of his native region. He loved his elder brother, whose premature death, in the Troad, occasioned the touching elegy of poem 101 and perhaps, by analogy, the consolatory lines of poem 96. There is no direct allusion anywhere to his feeling for his father or mother. Perhaps it is anachronistic to wonder whether or not he loved them. The Roman family was held together by traditional rights and duties rather than by the tenuous bonds of affection. However, one is tempted to see something of Baudelaire in the young poet: he had an appetite for the shocking. His ostentatious insolence towards Caesar suggests a certain desire to scandalise his father by attacking so boasted a guest. (It can equally be argued that there were good reasons for satirising Caesar apart from a wish to embarrass one's parents.) Baudelaire's outrageousness was, of course, directed especially against his step-father and the analogy should not be pressed with any vigour. However, the complexities of the Catullan psychology are perhaps at least made less 'inexplicable' in the light of the Baudelairean syndrome. For Catullus too seems to have pitched himself into a blatantly doomed relationship; he too had a certain fastidious *nostalgie de la boue.* That the object of his notorious passion was a woman of mature years, though scarcely old enough to be his mother, suggests (if such suggestions are illuminating) an Oedipal obsession. So too, though Catullus may sincerely have wished it otherwise, does his fidelity to a married woman notorious for her faithlessness. The hope that he could wrest Lesbia from her husband and from the way of life which she found so amusing may have been genuine enough. Passionate lovers are not in the habit of weighing the odds. Yet to hope, as he did, that he and Lesbia could ever be married, to hope even that she would cease to have other lovers, comes very close to the infantile fantasy that one's mother can become one's sole property, the father displaced from his own bed. Such psychological speculations neither tarnish nor explain the poetry which came of Catullus' eventually ruinous involvement, but they may enable us to see a unity behind the diversity of tone, style and content. Innocence and guilt, fastidiousness and coarseness, tenderness and perversity complement rather than contradict each other in the context of a passionate yet impossible love.

How could he ever have dedicated the purity of his feelings to an affair soon sordid with cynicism and betrayal? What may well have begun as a smart and casual affair - what better way to mark one's arival in smart society than by humping the hostess? - devloped into a dominating obsession. Even when he was supplanted in Lesbia's bed by his erstwhile friend, Caelius Rufus, he could not call it a day. He knew very well what sophisticated convention required - that one accept the transience of love with cynical grace - but he could not keep the rules, much as he may have wished to. Sensible men about Rome put such things down to experience and went on to the next adventure. Catullus was hooked. The apparently chic provincial poet, with his bold confidence in matters of aesthetics, fell victim to a naiveté he could wholly conceal, although he managed to ape the coolness of the in-crowd, to catch their tone and echo it in amusing squibs and sardonic epigrams which seemed to endorse their casualness in sexual matters. His own fervent fidelity to Lesbia did not entirely inhibit him from sexual indulgence in other directions, both with girls and with boys. The females were almost certainly professionals - Ameana and Ipsitilla (see poems 32 and 41) - whose charms were available when more sentimental satisfactions were denied, but the homosexual attachments, especially to Juventius, did not lack their emotional element. It may be said that we have no evidence that Catullus was literally involved with young men. Perhaps he was merely amusing himself by developing a standard erotic theme. The recommendation not to read biographical facts into a writer's work has led some critics to deny that there can be any inference at all from the text to the life. However, can anyone truly believe that Catullus did not actually love a woman whom he addresses as Lesbia but who was almost certainly the infamous Clodia? (T.P. Wiseman maintains in his essay *Lesbia - Who?* that it night as well have been her youngest sister,

16

who also had the hot blood of the family, but his agile arguments are not wholly convincing.) Catullus' poems are lively with the names of actual persons of the day and they would surely have had small point if they did not make equal play with their actual characters and actions. How can his accusation that Vibennius *père et fils* (poem 33) stole from the changing rooms in the public baths have been amusing unless it had some credible foundation in daily life? We should remember that Roman poetry was not written merely to be published but also to be performed; reading aloud was a standard part of poetic practice. Catullus and his clan undoubtedly competed in entertaining and dazzling one another. The reproaches which the anguished poet flings at his faithless friends (he seems to have been singularly ill-served) were not infrequently delivered to their faces, if they cared or dared to show them. The lighter poems in particular were intended to get laughs no less than to prick consciences. They can be best enjoyed, even today, by being spoken aloud. The sometimes abrupt changes of tone, even within the text of a short poem, make better sense if one presupposes an audience, rather than a solitary and silent reader. The dramatic or comic pause is part of the skilful machinery; the habit of taking Latin poetry as a printed text whose complexities must be construed and unravelled at an even, tortuous pace, has led generations of readers to miss the ironies which Catullus' implied timing was surely designed to emphasise. Often a twist in the last line turns solemnity to laughter, self-pity to self-deprecation.

An instance where the irony is usually missed is poem 35. The usual interpretation is that Catullus, the earnest critic, secretary-general of the *neoteroi*, writes to his friend Caecilius, who is some hundred miles away, and commands him at once to leave the girl whom he is enjoying in order to some post-haste to a literary

17

tutorial. Catullus has just read his friend's Ode dedicated to the Great Mother and wants to tell Caecilius what is wrong with it. Scholars have assumed the poem to be a serious summons, as if Catullus genuinely expected a young man (a young *Latin!*) to leap from his mistress's bed, having reminded her of Catullus' belief that poetry takes priority over love, and rush to be told what is wrong with his work. Well, of course Catullus took poetry seriously and of course that is one way of reading the poem. But it is precisely because Catullus and his friends did take their craft seriously that the lines also have a comic undertone. Surely they read more entertainingly as an ironic comment on Caecilius' affections of dedication to the Muse and also, perhaps, as an example of Catullan self-mockery: how can an inadequate poet like Caecilius be entitled to so enviably delicious a girl? Catullus presents himself here in the role, somewhat inverted, of Stevie Smith's Person From Porlock: he interrupts lovers with the news that a poem has to be worked out. Happiness, as Stevie Smith herself remarked, does not make us write, but rather puts thoughts of literature out of one's mind. The comedy of poem 35 lies in Catullus' confidence that Caecilius will *not* come. What comedy could have been left in it, had Catullus' audience seriously assumed that the dutiful lad would immediately obey his tutor's summons? There is a kind of final, tragic irony in the fact that Catullus himself, whose aesthetic convictions held poetry to be largely a matter of the intellect, proved no more able to abandon his mistress than was Caeilius. Here again the audience must have recognised how badly bitten was the biter. We are all good at enjoining sobriety on others, but who can be sure of his own?

Critics of Catullus have often emphasised the distinction between his sober and his scandalous self, without perhaps realising how closely they are linked. It seems incredible to certain prosaic people that Catullus can have been all *that* hurt by his wrecked affair with Lesbia. (The chronology is arguable - and argued about - but he seems to have been her official lover for a short time, during which they enjoyed the idyllic passion he naively imagined would endure forever. After that, he shared her favours for another period, before finally being excluded from them, either by his own belated nausea or by her decisive cruelty.) That he could have continued to be stricken three whole *years* after the collapse of his hopes may seem absurd to hard heads, but to imagine that a single affair cannot dominate a writer's thoughts for that long is to forget that Flaubert, for instance, loved Madame Schlésinger all his life, though he never shared her bed and only briefly her company. The imposition on himself of a rigorous system of impersonal literary endeavour in no way precluded Flaubert from an endless obsession with the woman of his dreams. 'Get over it' is precisely what writers so often cannot do. Affectations of tough-mindedness are often calculated to dissimulate embarrassingly persistent, even puerile softheartedness. Cynicism is sentiment that dare not speak its name. Somerset Maugham was notably beady-eyed in his attitude to the sexual and sentimental attachments of others, but he continued to weep over the death of his mother eighty years after the event; Proust's whole sense of life was coloured by the memory of a goodnight kiss. The sexual pathology of Catullus may now, at last, be discussed without false tact; such discussion is not necessarily more important than textual elucidation and need not be unduly prolonged, but it may help to establish an underlying unity which prudishness has obscured. It is generally held that the Lesbia poems are the sincere centre of the Catullan *oeuvre*. Some of them

19

are admittedly peripheral, like that alluding to Lesbia's brother, Lesbius (poem 79), the clearest evidence we have that Lesbia was indeed Clodia, the sister of that notorious Clodius whose appetite for scandal led him to dress up as a female and intrude on the ceremonies of the vestal virgins, thus breaking a taboo in a fashion which all decent Romans, however privately sceptical, were obliged to regard as sacrilegious. Clodia is widely believed to have committed incest with her racy brother, though the main evidence of this, apart from their dissolute reputations, comes from Cicero's speech *Pro Caelio,* in which he was defending Clodia's ex-lover and Catullus' ex-friend. It was essential to his case to blacken Clodia, which he seems to have done to such good effect that her name ceases to be mentioned in any chronicles of the period. Catullus' lampoon suggests that the rumour was generally current, though poem 79 too could be regarded as suspect on grounds of *parti pris*. However peripheral it may be, this little poem is the hinge, as it were, joining the 'sincere' side of Catullus, the side most agreeable to moralists, with the morally less sweet-smelling. For it needs no great psychological acuteness to see that Catullus was as much fascinated by betrayal as he was hurt by it. He was obsessed by Lesbia's lovers, about whom there is a considerable number of poems, particularly if one includes her husband among them. We need not regard these poems as symptoms of immaturity in order to see in them a psychological pattern which keeps step very well with the Oedipal syndrome. Catullus' 'confusion' - his inability to be 'grown-up', his incessant havering between one posture and another, between purity and lechery, hard and soft - makes singular sense if we admit that his sexuality was stimulated, however much it may have appalled him, by the very treachery which so painfully soured his love. Why does Catullus both love and hate? Why does he desire Lesbia more but love her less? The conflict between sex and love is less strange to us now than it was to generations of critics with little experience of life and reluctant powers of inferential self-analysis. Proust saw jealousy as the single greatest motive for love. If this view is exaggerated by his own sexual proclivities, it is surely one which enables us to understand Catullus better. Swann's love for Odette consumes the elegant cosmopolite no less thoroughly, and no less bewilderingly, than did love for Lesbia obsess Catullus; time and again Swann is aware that Odette is not really his type, but his dread of losing her, even when he has ceased to love her in the sentimental sense, makes him a slave to her moods. Jealousy replaces tenderness, but is almost more effective (and painfully tenacious) as an aphrodisiac. Herbert Gold's story *Love And Like* has a striking conclusion when a man, saying goodbye to the wife who is about to divorce him, is suddenly filled with a lust he has not felt for years and virtually rapes her. Many relationships are sustained by that kind of ambivalence. We diminish the complexity of Catullus' character, rather than preserve its integrity, when we choose to ignore the likely pattern of its emotional and sexual nature. Had Lesbia agreed to be as faithful as her lover's courtly side would have liked, had she honoured that notion of a true marriage he seemed so touchingly to desire, would their relationship really have prospered? What future in mundane fact could it ever have had? Clodia was a powerful woman, with a *salon* at the very centre of Roman political and social life. She had a complaisant and elderly husband (who died in 59 B.C.) and she pleased herself, as we have seen, with whatever man she fancied. Could Catullus ever seriously have supposed that she wanted to come and live with him in a country cottage? Even if it played a part in their amorous dialogue, one cannot see Clodia settling down for long to a life of well-water and rural *charcuterie*; even when Catullus seduces us, and convinces himself, most thoroughly with his idyllic visions, they remain manifestly illusory. His choice of Lesbia was, in some sense, perverse from the outset. She did not *become* impossible, but was always so. Was not that her attraction? For though there have indeed been cases in amorous history where sophisticated married ladies have been lured from a life of glittering cynicism, touched and sustained by the purity of their youthful lovers, Clodia was hardly a promising candidate for such redemption. She was too blatantly urban and urbane; to absent herself from her many felicities for the sake of a moon-struck poet, however many kisses he promised, or wanted, was virtually unthinkable. (Oddly enough, there is a vague literary parallel, an exception which hardly embarrasses the rule, in D.H. Lawrence's affair with Baroness von Richthofen, who was married, though in significantly more provincial and discontented circumstances, when the passionate young genius met and carried her off, though Frieda probably did quite as much of the carrying as Lawrence. Those who care to press analogies may diagnose in Catullus' urgent fervour the possibility that he, like Lawrence, was suffering from that frenzy for life which so often inflamed the tubercular.)

The enduring vitality of the Catullan *œuvre* is due not only to the genius of the poet, but also to the ageless immediacy of his predicament. He lends himself to translation both because he is a great poet and because his 'case', however particular and however unchallengeably unique in its original expression, has an undying call on our imaginations. The names of the woman he loved and of those he fucked, the men whom he trusted and who let him down, may bear an antique ring, but his situation has not dated at all. It may be that there are or will be societies where jealousy is unknown, where love and possessiveness have nothing in common, where Oedipus has no taste for Jocasta and where the eternal triangle, in all its contorted forms, is an unknown figure of speech or pattern of life, but until such a society is commonplace, the passion and anguish of Catullus will continue to seem abidingly modern. After that, his genius will have to work its own way with the reader; its chances of survival are unlikely to be very much impaired.

NOTE

The numbers of the poems follow those in Mynors' Oxford Text of 1958. (As there, poem 18 - fragmentary - and poems 19 and 20 - spurious - are omitted.) In a few cases, we felt that a poem could be 'registered' in two different ways: these have been numbered (i) and (ii).

The translation is throughout our joint responsibility. For each poem, one of us wrote a first draft, which the other revised; we then discussed and wrote the final version together.

We should like to acknowledge the help and encouragement, during our work on this translation, of Guy Lee, Kenneth Quinn, John Sullivan and Peter Green; also of Claire Stone, who typed many drafts.

1

Who's to be offered my brand-new slim volume
Slickly polished with dry-as-dust pumice-stone?
Cornelius, it's yours! After all, you always said
My little pieces had 'a modicum of merit'.
That to one side, you alone of Italy's sons has dared
To epitomise mankind in three instalments -
What style! What wit! What a performance!
Now take this offering of mine, for what it's worth,
And may my virgin mistress
Make it last, if only an aeon or two.

2

Well, little sparrow, who's my darling's darling, then?
Does she like to play with it and hold it in her lap?
Does she? Does she get it to stretch its beak
To tip her fingertip - provoke the little pecker's peck?
My shining love, my own glittering passion -
Does she sometimes have a little game? Does she?
I'm told she does. I'm told she has no time
For serious feelings, lets them all go hang.
And a sparrow helps a bit. Tell me little sparrow,
When can I play with you as she does
And have you unload my heart? Tell me -
I'll look as sharp as that sharp girl (they say)
When a little golden apple came along
And undid her, undid her belt, her girdle,
And pushed her over, at last, into love's free zone.

25

3

Come, join the mourners; come, Gods of Love,
Gods of desire; come, whoever loves Venus first
And join the dirge. Death has struck my love.
Her sparrow's dead. My darling's darling,
Dead, who knew his mistress better than a girl
Her mother. He was never out of her lap,
Jumping here, jumping there, jumping back again!
As soon as he saw her, up he piped and piped
For no one else. Now it's over forever.
Down that dark tunnel he's gone, from where, they
    say,
Once vanished, you never rise again.
The hell with you, you shades of Hell.
You get us all down in the end,
Even the most beautiful. Beautiful sparrows
You won't even spare us. It's cruel.
It's murder; that poor little bird!
In passing, sparrow, do you know
That you went and made Lesbia cry?
Her eyes are red-rimmed and puffy.
You've actually made them look *small*.

4

That far-sailing craft you see, my friends,
Silly at anchor was once, if you believe it,
The slickest thing afloat. Aye, it insists:
No log in all the world can claim
It was ever overtaken: oar or canvas
Makes no odds. She goes further -
Dares the pouting Adriatic say otherwise,
Or the Cyclades, island by island;

26

Rhodes - *noblesse oblige* - will bear her out,
And the bristling Propontis (Thracian branch);
Even surly Pontus ought to own it's true.
After all, she hails from there:
What became a streamlined clipper
Used to bear a full head of leaves
On a high Cytorean ridge.
Where do you think she learned
To hiss at the passing wind?

Amastris on the Pontus - Cytorus, boxed with trees -
Come back: you're called as referees.
She says you know her, intimately too -
In fact, she claims descent from the highest
In the land, this crafty character,
And swears she dipped virgin oars
Into your very waters.

The rest was easy: she bore her owner
Through seas never high enough
To touch him, forget how the wind was blowing -
From the left, the right, even (by Jove!) in the centre.
Never an S.O.S. to the Gods on shore,
Not from the day she first wet her keel
Till she limped to a last anchorage,
In the lake, right here. Or that's her story.
Now she's a quiet old lady,
With only the sky to sail,
And she gives way at last to you, twin Castor -
And equally to Castor's twin.

5

We can live, my Lesbia, and love.
What do you mean, people are talking?
Asinine rumours, old husbands' tales;
You could mount their wits on a farthing.
The sun rises (they tell us); the sun sets,
Rises and sets again. But not for you and me:
For us it happens once. Our day dies;
Night comes, and in that night we sleep
Forever. So, for ever, kiss me now.
A thousand, so . . . a hundred, good . . .
Another thousand, and a hundred more . . .
Another thousand . . . hundred . . . thousand . . .
We *must* do it over and over -
It's obvious - surely you see?
If even we lose track of the figures,
No one can tax us for loving at all.

6

Flavius, this little dish of yours -
Out with it, tell me the truth:
When am I going to meet her?
She's on the plain side of dumb,
Am I right? If I'm wrong,
What's keeping you so quiet?
All right, she's a hot-cunted whore, then -
She must be, I tell you, or else
You'd have let it out by now.
You're not spending your nights alone,
Now are you?
There's too much noise in your room
(And a strong smell of Syrian musk).

Just take a look at your bolster:
It's shagged out, even if you aren't.
Your bed's got the shakes as well -
Presumably overwork.
So you might as well spill it now:
Give us your side of the story.
Why? You're clapped out, that's why -
Or have you some other limp excuse?
What's she like, man? Come on!
What? What business of mine? Poetic, of course:
I'm poised to sing praises of passion
That can ride up to heaven on high.
Or I could just send you up instead.

7

Your questions, Lesbia, are these:
(a) How many kisses to sate
(b) How many to surfeit my passion?

Answer: go to Cyrene
And count the grains of Libya's sand -
Yes, the whole lasarpiciferous* desert.
Begin where Jupiter breathes hot tips
For his oracle's Ammonian branch
And count on going to old Battus' tomb
(He founded the place, you'll recall).

Or: go number the numberless stars
That look down in the wordless night
On men that are out to steal kisses.
To kiss you as often as that

*It means: bearing an alliaceous fruit.

Would suffice any normal madman
And possibly one called Catullus.

As many as not the peepingest Tom
Could keep up with - a number too fat
To get any envious tongue around.

8

Catullus, Catullus, Catullus,
You're being a fool. So stop.
What's dead is dead. Now face it.
Once the sun shone full upon you, once.
Her wish was your desire. We know.
Wish? Desire? I loved her
As no woman will ever be loved.
If she was happy, you were happy -
What you wanted, she came to want it too.
We know. The sun shone full upon you.
Now she wants no more to do with you
And there's nothing more you can do.
Why run after what's already run out?
Or live with your face in your hands?
Put her out of your mind. Don't weaken. Forget.
I tell you, tell her *Goodbye*. That's it.
Catullus seen doing the obvious thing.
Mouth shut; ears shut. Finished. All right?
Oh but oh she'll be sorry
When no one comes wanting her love.
Bitch, bitch, for the rest of your life
Who's going to bother, quite frankly,
To tell you how lovely you are?

Whom will you love? Who'll have you then?
And then what about kisses?
Whose lips will you bite in the end?
Catullus, Catullus, remember: forget.

9

Veranius, I'm not short of friends:
I've got exactly three hundred thousand;
It just so happens you're number one.
Is it true you're back home again
With your old mother and those brothers
Who love you one hundred per cent?
It's true? You're safe? That's great.
And when do I get to see you,
And to hear all your usual nonsense -
Who's who and what's what in Spain?
I'm coming over, yes, right now,
To fall on your neck like a lover
And kiss you hullo on the mouth, on the eyes.
I mean it; I couldn't be happier;
I'm the happiest man in the world.

10

Friend Varus nabs me down in the Forum
(Where I'm busily hanging about):
I must come and meet her, he says.
Meet who? His latest tart, of course -
It didn't take long to see that.
Not bad either: nice taste, nice tits:
So far so good. But then we talk.

We talk about this, we talk about that.
Bithynia comes up. How did I do there?
What was it like? How were the pickings?
'Not a soul made a penny I heard of,
Not in the heavy or the light brigade.
No palms were greased, no heads patted -
How could they be, with H.E. on top?'
(That bugger was always on top.)
'Rubbish!' they said. 'Bithynian
Bearers - surely you picked up a set
Of those?' Well, what could I say?
I had to give her the works.
'All right, so I did have some luck -
I'm not quite as green as I look.
Eight of them came back with me - eight
Upstanding lads with good hard backs.'
That was my story. But you know me,
I haven't one, not even to carry
A chairleg across the room, or back.
It took her in, of course
(I said she was easily had).
'O Catullus, do be a love,
Let me give them a canter - say
Up to the East End and back?'
What can you do with girls like that?
'Hold it,' I said, 'Let me finish.
They're Cinna's, not mine - and you know Gaius,
His, mine, what's the difference?
I use them as if they were mine.
Must you be so literal minded?
You made me stick my neck right out,
And now I've tripped over my tongue.'

11

Aurelius and Furius, dear friends,
Let's take a trip together - all the way
To India, perhaps, where all land ends
    In fretting, foaming sea;
To far Hyrcania, Arabia gay;
To arrow-darting Parthia; to see
The Sagans, or that wide Egyptian bay
    The seven-mouthed Nile stains brown;
We'll struggle up the Alps (you follow me?)
And on the topmost tips stand looking down
On mighty Caesar's monuments; we'll free-
    wheel down the Rhine, and then
We'll cross the bristling sea to Britain - town
By ghastly town, my friends, like gallant men
We'll sample every one. But first, don't frown
    When asked to see that bitch
I used to love; go seek her out again
And tell her this from me: that itch
Of hers, good luck to it! Good scratching, when
    She mounts three hundred pricks
At once, and fills that ever-gaping niche
That once was mine, and cracks their balls for kicks.

I drooped and fell for her, like an evening flower
Cut by a heedless plough, dead in an hour.

12

Asinius Marrucinus! Yes, you:
I saw what your left hand was doing.
When everyone's laughing and drinking,
You whip your hosts' napkins for fun.
I presume it's supposed to be funny;
In fact it's just crummy and cheap.
Exaggerating am I? Ask Pollio.
He'd give a fortune to have you change.
Since your brother has charm and wit,
He doesn't stoop to stealing his laughs.
Look, do you want another instalment,
300 memory-jogging lines? No?
Then send back my napkin, express.
It's nothing to do with the money:
It reminds me of absent friends,
Being part of some Spanish linen
Fabullus and Veranius sent.
And as they are people I do love,
I feel keenly about that napkin as well.

13

You're going to eat like a king, Fabullus,
At my house in a couple of days -
Assuming the Gods send you well,
And assuming you bring the supplies.
(Quality and quantity, please):
First, a delicious girl -
And wine and wit and a fresh catch of laughs.
Pick them up on your way, lover boy,
And you'll not go short of a feast.
Am I out of funds, did you ask?

My dear chap, my wallet is bulging:
Bulging with cobwebs.
Will you accept a draught of love?
Or - no pro quo could be quidder than this -
A dab of my mistress's secret scent
(Exclusive, from Venus, Cupid and co.).
One sniff and you're down on your knees,
Praying to the Gods, Fabullus,
To make all your faculties nose.

14 a

Calvus, you charming young bastard,
I'm in receipt of your gift.
If I didn't love you more than my eyes,
I'd hate you for it, my dear:
Same hatred you keep for Vatinius.
What did I do, what can I have said
To merit such measures against me?
The Gods should punish the toady
Who sent you such ungodly junk.
But if - and I have my suspicions -
They came from a well-known source -
Sulla, anthologist, pundit and critic,
All right, I'll do my good deed for the day,
If it saves you wasting your time.
Gods, what unspeakable rubbish!
A token of friendship, you say?
I've wasted my whole Saturnalia,
My favourite day of the year.
No, smarty, you shan't get away with it:
I'll be up as soon as it's light
And down to the second-hand stalls.
Any Caesius? Any Aquinus? Suffenus?

I'll make up a poisonous package
And pay you back for your pains.
As for you lot, be off, false quantities all,
Limp home on your wretched club-feet.
'Signs of the critical times!'
Bloody awful poets, that's what.

14 b (i)

Readers, do you plan to be readers of mine?
If my little efforts amuse you,
Might I suggest? Don't ever flinch
From applause.

14 b (ii)

So readers, you think you'll get a rise
From what I have to offer? Fine:
Stretch out your hands, take hold . . .

15

Myself and the one I love, Aurelius,
I put under your protection.
So grant me this modest favour:
If ever you have wanted
To keep just one thing chaste
(Or even roughly pollution-free),
Keep this young man so for me.
I don't mean just from the plebs -
They don't bother me much.

A virgin's safe in the rush-hour:
No room to mix business with pleasure.
Quite frankly, it's you that I fear:
You prick, you've a hard reputation -
You've got it in for all the boys.
As far as I'm concerned, keep it up,
Wherever, whoever you like,
As long as it's not around here.
Look, one simple exception:
In my view, it isn't a lot.
So: if you get any nasty ideas,
You sod, and dare to get cracking
(Tempting that soft head into your noose),
I give you a solemn warning:
You'll wish you'd had a different end.
I'll lash you up with the door open
And stuff your back passage with fish
(Mullet garnished with radishes),
Prescribed suppository.

16

Bugger you and likewise sucks,
Aurelius who stoops and Furius who stabs.
So you deduce from my little verses -
Which I concede to be 'pretty indecent' -
That I am pretty and indecent too?
A true poet must be pure and devoted;
His work is another thing.
It gives a poem wit and attack
To be a little bit juicy
And not invariably nice.
I like a line that gives one a lift.
Youth hardly needs such a service,

But why not a leavening prod
For hairy old sods with ponderous cocks
Who don't find it easy to rise?
So you've read of my thousands of kisses
(Bestowed on a girl, as you know),
And now you call me less than a man?
Well, bugger you, as I hinted above,
And when that's over, sucks.

17

Wanted by the town of Colonia:
A reliable span for a great, long bridge.
The old worlde one is arthritic,
Rickety, lurching on second-hand crutches:
Who's going dancing on *that*?
'We don't want our fête's name to be mud!'
Right: build whatever bridge you fancy -
Go to whatever lengths you need -
Test it with jackboots, morris-men, can-cans.
But 'prior to building permission'
Give me the nod for one final laugh.
There's one particular Colonial
I'd love to see in it, right up to his neck,
Right there where the stuff is thickest
And has a characteristic nose.
They don't come much thicker than chummy:
He hasn't the brains of a baby
Nodding on Dadda's arm. He's married
A very young girl, green as a bud
At its greenest, frisky as a kid
(But you know how goats can develop).
Kid-glove treatment is just what she needs,
Handling you'd give a quality grape.

He lets her do as she likes, and guess
What she likes to do! He must have piles:
He never gets off his arse.
He might as well be a log, sawn off
At the root in some Ligurian ditch.
He knows as much about what she's at
As if he'd never had her. Sans eyes,
Sans ears, doesn't know if he's coming
Or going, or even if he can.
That's my candidate to go flying.
I thought the shock of walking the plank
Might do wonders for stick-in-the-muds.
I'm hoping he'll shed his narcosis:
Cf. mules shedding shoes in a bog.

21

Aurelius, you king of eaters out,
Today, yesterday, tomorrow too,
The one I love, you fancy. There's no doubt:
You don't exactly hide it, do you?
You're both one big laugh, and in public.
(So *that's* what's meant by sticking to it!)
You greedy sod, you don't miss a trick.
But all in vain, if you did but know it.
So you've scored first, you've got a head start -
Well, I shall come from behind, my dear.
If you'd acted from fullness of heart,
I'd be silent. As it is, I fear
Your appetites in meat and drink
Infect my lover. Here appended
My advice: stop sensibly and think,
Or be literally upended.

22

Your old friend Suffenus is at it again,
Varus. Agreed, he's nobody's fool,
Has charm, talks well, knows his way around,
And writes by far the longest verses in the world,
Ten thousand lines - revised, what's more -
Unless I counted wrong. Unabridged texts:
He's not heard of the paper shortage.
Crown octavo, quality parchment;
Stiff endpapers, flashy bindings,
Tailor-made linen jackets, the lot
Hand-ruled and polished to perfection.
Then comes the reading. And *then* where's
The charm, the sophistication?
He bleats; he hacks. You'd reckon his line
Was milking goats or digging ditches.
Talk about bad! What a change was there!
I mean, can you explain why smartyboots -
Or whatever is smarter than that -
Becomes rustier than a rustic
The moment he fingers a dactyl?
Yet he's never so happy as then:
He's in heaven: Narcissus the poet!
Oh, I daresay we're all much the same.
Who isn't some kind of Suffenus
Somewhere along the line? Everyone's
Blind to what's there, on his own spine.

23

From Furius: 'I haven't a penny,
Not a servant to my name, nothing.'
Well, you haven't got fleas either.
'Not a spider, not a spark in the grate.'
Then be grateful: you live with Daddy
And dear old Daddy's second wife.
You sit and split rocks with your teeth.
What with your pater and his lady
(Your step-mother's the original
Chip off the old block) you've got it
Made: the cushiest *ménage-à-trois*.
If you're skint, what can be the problem?
No call for the fire brigade,
No wear and tear, no burglars
After the family portraits, no danger
From poisonous heirs: you're covered
By nature's All Risks Policy!
Your bodies (God knows) are dry as bones;
And if you want a dustier image,
What is there drier than dry?
The sun? Ten degrees of frost?
Or might I venture - deliberate greed?
Oh do go and count your blessings:
No sweat; nose never blocked;
No saliva; no sinusitis.
In fact, your refinement's finer still:
Salt would run smooth from your arse-hole.
You don't crap ten times in a year;
And when you do, it's baked beans
And issues in pebble form.
Rub it between the fingers
And they come up smelling of roses.
You've got the perfect set-up,
And you need 'ten thousand, cash'?
My dear, don't push your luck.

24

Flosculus I call you, little flower, floweret,
(Later: the part of the fruit where the blossom was),
Pride and ornament of the Juventii,
Of this and past and future generations;
I'd sooner you gave him the touch that Midas had
Than let him touch you, the one I'm thinking of.
He's never a servant, nowhere (*arca*) to put his
    treasure.
Don't let him be your lover, will you, ever?
'Why? Isn't he a handsome fellow?' Yes indeed.
A handsome fellow with never a servant and nowhere
To put his treasure (*arca*). Yes indeed.
If that's your pleasure, chuck me over
And hoist him up. Give him a servant
And somewhere to put his treasure.

25

Thallus, you very bad fairy,
Softer than a rabbit's furry,
Softer than *pâté de foie gras*,
Softer than an ear-lobe you are;
Boneless as a spider's skein is
Or an old man's mingy penis;
Thallus, you're a grabbing whirlwind
When Sloth, your Goddess, has a mind
To lull the witnesses to sleep
And lets you play the thief, you drip.
Send back that cloak you filched of mine
And my Saetaban napkins from Spain,
And my Bithynian primitives
(You claim those wogs as *relatives*?).

Give, sticky fingers; send 'em back -
Or do limp wrist and downy flank
Fancy the scoring of the lash?
(Yes, nether cheeks can also blush.)
You'll leap about like a baby boat
Caught out at sea by a wind distraught.

26 (i)

The South Wind never lashes it,
The North Wind never bashes it,
Nor dust from East, nor rain from West:
Furius has a cosy nest.
Meets no draught, safe from every quarter -
Save every quarter when he ought to
Cover his banker's draft again.
Furius gets the wind up then.

26 (ii)

The South Wind never lashes it,
The North Wind never bashes it,
Nor dust from East, nor rain from West:
Furius, mine's a cosy nest.
Meets no draught, safe from every quarter -
Save every quarter when I ought to
Cover my banker's draft again.
I really get the wind up then.

27

Waiter, you with the keys
To the little old Falernian!
Bring in a case of the hard stuff,
As Postumia's law lays down.
(She's judiciously more juiced
Than the very juiciest grape.)
All mineral waters - out!
You only blight the wine.
Go piss on the Catos' doorsteps.
This here (hic) is Domaine de Bacchus.
I propose to drink it neat.

28

Well well, so now you're Piso's men?
You flabby pair: you always travel light.
There's no snugger-fitting, no emptier bag
Than yours, Veranius dear, or yours,
Fabullus. How goes every little thing?
Hungry business, soldiering, is it?
Chilblains making you complain?
What? Piso's a pisser, you say?
So: write your memoirs and flog 'em,
Like I did with my C.O.
Baby, I was screwed into the ground
By Memmius, and took it lying down.
I felt every inch of that yard of his:
He took his pleasures slowly, that one.
And now *you're* getting shafted
By a prick of much the same bore.
Well, you asked for it: you wanted classy friends!
Every possible bad luck to you both,
You spotted dicks, end of the Roman line.

44

29

Who can stand and look at it?
Who can look and stand it?
A rooting pig, I suppose,
And a dicey one at that.
Unspoiled Gaul despoiled,
Distant Britain poached!
Rome, you're fucked, but can you stand it?
Look: he's always on the rise;
He's coming up - first storey high.
Or do you fancy him cock-of-the-walk?
Are you ready to call him Adonis?
O Romulus, even in drag
Can you really fancy that?
A rooting pig, I call him,
And a dicey one at that.

Was it for this, O generalissimo,
That you marched
To the westest isle of them all?
Was it your strategic plan
That a clapped-out prick like this
Should piss away your millions?
An unusual use of funds!
Hasn't he got through enough
One way and another?
Have you ever watched him at table?
First course: his old man's goodies.
Second: the meat of the Pontic wars.
Third: fresh from the Spanish campaign,
The golden fruits of the Tagus.
No wonder Britain and Gaul
Are shaking like table jellies.

Why in hell do you stand it?
He'd never have downed it all
Without help. You two
Supplied the softening sauce,
Caesar and Pompey, well-known double-act.
Was Mamurra's the name on your scutcheons
When you pulled the plug on the world?

30

What *can* you remember, Alfenus,
When you forget your own best friends?
One must be realistic, you say,
You've got no time for regrets.
I was 'the sweetest thing in your life',
But you're letting me go regardless;
You haven't a qualm, you say.
Liars don't get away with lying:
The Gods come down heavily on it.
Had you forgotten that, in your haste
To be shot of my 'miserable moaning'?
Tell me, what ought one to do next?
Where can I put my trust?
You weren't short of words, I must say,
When you wanted me 'next to your heart'!
Everything was going to be fine.
Weren't those roughly your words?
Bastard. Now you take it all back.
What you said, what you did: all kaput.
Gone with the wind. I'm given the air.
My dear, *you* may have forgotten;
But the gods still remember,
And honour remembers too.
You'll be damned sorry one day
For what you did, and what you do.

31

Of every place that's all-but island, Sirmio,
Of all islands too, the peach,
As many as Neptune-bitter/Neptune-sweet
Holds out on brimming lake or flowing sea,
How I've lusted for you - and how! Glad to see you?
A pause: for believing my eyes.
Goodbye to jolly old 'thynia
And those B- thynian marches. Me. You. Here. Safe.
Oh what's more heaven than this,
To be done with doing one's duty?
Wit sheds its uniform: we're through
With diplomatic bags, and home, my God, we're home.
Oh my lucky stars, to nod off in a bed that fits: beat
   that!
Down payment for services rendered.
How goes it with you, my pretty little Sirmio?
Where's a smile for a smiling master?
And what can you do, lake of Lydian wave
(My Etruscan compliments to you?)
Cackle out loud, as much as you like:
Waves of laughter for lovers caught in the act.
Catullus and Sirmio at it. He he he he he.

32

Intention: love.
My dear sweet Ipsitilla,
My pet, you're the very girl:
Have me report to you this pip emma.
If the answer's Roger, be sure
(a) No one bolts your door before I do
(b) You don't get an itch to go roaming.

I want you indoors,
With nine complete plans of campaign.
The exercise? Fucking by numbers.
So: if you're on, send a runner.
I've had my hot meal and I'm in the picture:
Lying here stiff at attention
Bashing holes in my Number One Dress.

33

Bracketed top of the league,
Changing-room thieves' division,
Vibennius father and sod of a son
(The old man's a right shit,
The boy's arse-hole pinches things too),
Why not take a one-way ticket
To some far from salubrious shore?
It is, as of now, time to scarper:
Dad, you're facing serious charges -
Everybody in town knows that -
And as for you, sonny boy,
The market's fallen out of your bottom.

34

To Diana are we pledged,
We boys and girls unfledged;
May she our song inspire,
Pure boys and girls in choir.

Leto's great child we love,
Daughter of greatest Jove;

Propped 'gainst an olive tree,
In Delos she bore thee,

To be of hills the queen
And woodlands turning green;
In magic groves you hide
And booming rivers ride.

Mothers call you midwife:
'Juno, from pain bring life!'
Trivia, warlock, your names,
And moon with sun-filched flames.

Goddess, your monthly course
Gives years their driving force:
The farmer's crude abode
With healthy fruits you load.

Be called whate'er you please,
We pray you without cease
To keep a smiling face
For Romulus' good race.

35

To a lyric poet and fellow-spirit,
To Caecilius, papyrus, pray post
And bid him come to Verona.
He's to skip the walls of Como
And say farewell to his Larian lake.
Criticism time: points from a mutual friend!
So it's a hundred and thirty miles -
A picnic for a man of his sap.
What's this? A smashing girl's charms

To magic him out of leaving?
A thousand arms around his neck,
Begging him, please, to stay his step?
So it's true, frustration's raging
Since she read the work in hand?
'*Dindymi dominam* . . .' She caught fire
From the passionate poem;
She's been burning inside ever since.
That's no criticism, my dear:
You've responses sharper than Sappho's.
And I agree, Caecilius' Ode
Has the most seductive beginning -
But how, Magna Mater, does it end?

36

Volusius, your Annals - shit on paper,
But what a service they can render!
Lesbia's sworn a silly oath;
And they can help her off the hook.
It's to Venus and to Cupid:
If Catullus will come to his senses -
i.e. cease his vicious tum titty tumming -
She'll sacrifice the foulest of poets,
Personally anthologised,
To the God whose feet don't scan.
The muck to be burned on faggots
No less benighted than he.
Naughty girl, she fancied her wit
Would tickle that ticklish pair.
Let it pass; here's the kiss-off:
'Oh Goddess born of the blue, blue sea,
Hallowed Ida is home to Thee,
And Urii where the winds do blow,

Ancon and reedy Cnidus Thou dost know,
Amathus and Golgi and Dyrrachium
(Where the Adriatic's bread comes from);
Stamp now our debt as paid,
Mark my lady's vow as laid.'
Not uncharmingly put, I trust;
One so wants to be lovely to Love.
Come on now. Into the flames with you, quick!
Yes, Volusius, your Annals -
Shit in hexameter form.

37

Sexpothouse altogetherboys,
Ninth pillar up from the Brothers,
Woolworth dimeadozenhouse,
The only ones with big ones, eh?
So we're all armpit, are we?
Lickhairy gangbang all the girls,
Altogetherboys all in a row,
Sit-tight assarses bunched up there,
A hundred of you? Two? No sweat:
I'll get right in there amongst you,
One quickprick allabuggering together,
And badge the house with your testimonials:
Soppy dicks, the slickquickpricks.
She loved me once, loved and left me once,
The girl I loved as nevermore another,
The girl I fought and fought and fought for -
And now she can't resist you, eh?
Sexpotluck: come one, come all.
You all come to her in the end,
Even (and it's pitiful, pitiful)
Backstreet bumboys second-class,

And Egnatius the king of them all,
Egnatius! Mrs Warren's favourite son,
Cunticulous Celtiberian
Pisselegance, dentipricks incarnate -
So you're in, Dago Division Number One?

38

How goes it with dear Catullus?
Badly, Cornificius, badly.
Were Hercules me, he'd be labouring;
And it's getting rougher,
Rougher all the time. So what
Are you doing about it?
Not a drop of the corniest solace,
Not a tiny apostrophe.
Angry? I am angry.
Call yourself a friend?
Concoct some lines to weep me dry,
A la Simonides.

39

Egnatius has got white teeth.
And he does flash them everywhere.
A big case: counsel winding up,
Jury in tears.
                E's grinning, ear to ear.
A cremation: only son, a paragon;
Sobbing mother, inconsolable.
E's grinning, ear to ear.

                    Always,
Never mind what, when, where,
He flashes.
                Gods, how he flashes!
It's sick.
              He thinks it's smart.
I don't.
              He thinks it's Rome.
                              It's not.
Somebody should tell him? Let me.
Sonny, suppose you belonged in Rome,
Or were Sabine or Tiburtine,
Raw Umbrian, Etruscan lardo,
A Lanuvine (spade face, donkey teeth),
Or from over the Po (one of my ain folk);
Suppose you were anybody
Who cleaned his teeth *au point* . . .
I'd still say no,
                no,
                      no flashing.
What's more putting-off than put-on smiles?
But,
      señor,
              you're a Dago, and we know
In Dagoland urine's your dentifrice.
A gargle to ginger the gingiva.
So,
      the spicker his span shines tonight,
The more E's pissed the previous night.

Cheese?

40

What crazy idea, dear Ravidus,
Makes you collide with Catullus?
Whose name have you taken in vain
That he's sending you raving mad?
Or is it just public relations?
Well? Making a name for yourself?
You will. Unless you lay off my love,
I'll scribble my lines on your back
And you can quote me.

41

Ameana, that public amenity,
Has sent me a final demand:
Not one thousand: ten!
A pickle-nosed piece like that,
Sucking the cock of Formiae dry.
Oh but how can you be so callous?
Quick, call her friends, call a doctor -
She's gone raving mad:
'Mirror, mirror on the wall . . .'
Not a question she'd normally ask.

42

Calling all hendecasyllables, come in,
All hendecasyllables: emergency!
Look who's holding me up as a joke. Miss Fuck-face.
She says no, she won't give me back my work in hand.
Are you going to stand for it? After her:

Keep asking. She doesn't often say no twice.
Whom do I mean? You can't miss her. There she is,
Cruising along - note the professional walk
And the smirk, like a wolfcub crossed with a frog.
Get round her, altogether boys, in chorus:
'You stinking whore, hand over that manuscript!
Hand over, you stinking whore - the manuscript!'
Not on your arse? The shit, the walking whorehouse!
We shall have to find something ruder to say.
We've done enough already? I don't agree . . .
Well? No new ideas? At least make her *blush*,
The bitch, and take the smile off her face.
Altogether now, *fortissimo*, same again.
'You stinking whore, hand over that manuscript!
Hand over, you stinking whore - the manuscript!'
Nothing. We're getting nowhere. She isn't budging.
I propose a change of tone, and of tactics.
See if a variant reading does any good:
'Fair lady and chaste - hand over the fucking
    manuscript!'

43

Here comes our leading lady now!
Isn't that the cutest nose you ever saw?
No, it isn't.
                Hasn't she a beautiful walk?
No.
        The dark eyes, the slender hands!
I don't see any.
                The lips . . .
                                Need wiping.
The *voice*!

Do you think it's particularly nice?
Her friend was once Mr Big (in Formiae).
RAVE RECEPTION ON PROVINCIAL TOUR.
'Beats Lesbia,' say pundits.
                                    Pundits!
Generation of zeros: no standards, no style.

44

To my farm . . .
                        (Is it Sabine or Tiburtine?
They call it Tiburtine who rate Catullus smart;
To see him smart, the rest lay odds on Sabine.)
Be you Sabine or - more like it - Tiburtine,
What a health farm you've proved to be.
I've cleared my chest of a beastly cough,
Which I asked for and my stomach gave me,
Greedy for fancy invitations.
Imagine, I wanted to dine with Sestius.
So I get hold of his campaign speech
v. Antius. Pure poison. Chilling stuff.
I gulp it down. Result? Thick head, hacking cough.
I ran, shaking, to you, like a mother's breast
And found my cure - just sleep and nettle tea.
Wherefore, I render most hearty thanks.
I was a fool and you didn't tax me for it.
Hence I solemnly swear: all further draughts
Of his sickening muck shall go to S. direct
(Enclosed find cough and cold), no more to me.
Forget 'Do read it and then we'll dine':
He turns my stomach before he feeds it.

45

Acme in Septimius' lap: *The Kiss*
Made flesh. Hugging her close, he says, 'Acme,
My sweet perfection, I'm lost in loving you;
I'll love you always, till the end of time
Or even longer. It's true: I swear it!
If I'm wrong, may I come, alone in Africa
Or sunburned India, on a tawny lion . . .'
   That's what he said. And Cupid sneezed
   (Right and Left) good luck: God bless you, both.
Then Acme, leaning her light head back,
Gentled her darling's love-besotted eyes
With kiss-bruised lips, and said, 'My dear,
My life, my Septimillus, let's enslave
Ourselves to love, and love alone,
For ever - as keen as this keen flame
That makēs my breast a furnace . . .'
   That's what she said. And Cupid sneezed
   (Right and Left) good luck: God bless you, both.
So, blessed and happy, off they sail
On a voyage of mutual adoration.
Septimius (look!) has chosen Acme
Over all her Syrian or Britannic sisters;
Acme swears she'll live for him alone,
In him find all love's sweet varieties.

Has anyone ever seen a happier couple?
Anyone a Venus more benign?

46

Now spring, cold-banishing, brings back warmth.
Now the temper of the equinoctial sky
Grows calmer. The West Winds freshen:
Time to quit Phrygia, young Catullus,
And the fat fields of fever-hot Nicaea;
Let's be off to places that figure on the map,
Big names out here. Big thrill!
One longs to be gone; light feet itch for the road.
But where's the happy band of fellow-travellers
Who left together on the long road from home?
Different, parting ways take us back again.

47

Porky and Pig-face (cut-price Socrates),
Left-hand men of Piso, Messrs Itch and Scratch,
So you, and not my well-beloved Veranius and Fabullus,
Come first with that blunt prick Piso?
You put on your dinner jackets after lunch
And make a day of it, while my old friends
Stand on corners and ply for hand-outs.

48

Honey-sweet eyes are yours, Juventius.
Imagine: leave granted for up to X kisses!
Up to a thousand (times 300) could I give
And never look like being satisfied.
Not if thicker than stiff-standing wheat
Rose the harvest of kissings, yours and mine.

49 (i)

Most most eloquent of all the sons of Romulus,
Of those that are, and have been - Marcus Tullius -
And will be in future years.
Catullus, worst of all poets,
Tenders you his grateful, grateful thanks.
As much the worst of all poets is he
As you are best of all speakers.

49 (ii)

Most skilful in speaking on a subject of Romulus'
    grandsons,
As many as exist and have existed - Marcus Tullius,
    who else? -
And as many as will exist in other times,
Thanks to you, of the most effusive kind, Catullus
Hereby assigns to you, he the worst of all poets.
If he is the worst of all poets,
You are the best of all advocates, of all possible causes.

50

Yesterday, Calvus, was one to treasure;
We improvised, as children play, for pleasure:
Whole notepads full! And *weren't* we naughty boys?
Scribbling doggerel, matching words like toys;
You chose a metre, then the choice was mine,
Idyllic games, pouring out jokes - and wine.
And then when the time came for me to quit,
Glowing with your rhyme and roasted by your wit,

My excitement no evening meal could calm,
Nor would sleep my *darling eyes* seal with balm.
All night, restless, raging hot I lay
Versifying, and longing for the day
When with you I could be again and play.
Lying exhausted on my wretched bed,
Sprawled out, written out, more or less half dead,
This poem, my sweet, this a.m. I penned
To show you what you've done to me, my friend.
Reject not harshly my invitation
Nor cap it, dear heart, with deprecation.
Nemesis might come and claim a forfeit;
She can be a bitch - so just come off it!

51

Godlike he seems
Or (blasphemy!) higher still
Who sits with you,
    Sees you, hears you
Softly laugh - oh, Lesbia,
That laugh. It tears
My senses. Sweet, when
    First I saw you,
All speech died; tongue thick,
Ears pounding, eyes
Dark, limbs drenched
    In trickling fire.
No ease, Catullus: ease
Makes you edgy,
Irritable; ease destroyed
    Old kings, high towns.

52

What are you waiting for, Catullus?
                    Suicide time.
To the chair of honour comes Nonius Struma:
                    Scrofulous tumour.
'As sure as I'll be consul,' swears Vatinius.
                    The perjurer gives his word.
Catullus, what are you waiting for?
                    Suicide time.

53

I had to laugh. A nobody in the gallery
Hearing our Calvus in full flow
In re Vatinius, his iniquities,
Holds up his hands (amazement) and observes,
'Heavens, can't the little bugger talk?'

54

OTHO: PRICK-HEAD, SMALLEST ON THE MARKET.
HIRRUS: MANURE HALFWAY UP HIS LEG, COUNTRYMAN.
IT'S HEADY, IT'S CHEAP, IT'S LIBO'S FART.
Could you please be disgusted by these,
Great Caesar, if by nothing else? (Throw in
Fufidius - old man seeking youth in a stew.)
No? It's my verses that make you angry?
They don't deserve it, Caesar . . . Caesarissimo.

55

A humble request, if you're not too busy:
Where the hell are you hiding these days?
We've had search-parties out in the park;
Ditto the Circus and the bookshops
And hallowed ground (Jove's on Capitol Hill).
I did a personal walkabout myself,
And polled the ladies round Pompey's Porch.
All wide-eyed innocence, they stared, the whores;
But I plugged on, of course. 'Camerius,
Come on, beauties, what've you done with him?'
One of them made a clean breast of it:
'Here he is, between my pretty titties, hiding,
Have a look!'
      Hercules would have a job
Keeping up with you. You've gone too far
This time, denying us your lordship's sight.
At least name a time and a place. Come on.
Courage, *avanti*, don't be shy!
It's a harem of platinum blondes, am I right?
Look, persist in this dumb insolence
And you're junking the best of the fruit.
Venus likes a man who can kiss *and* tell.
Oh well, if you insist, stay buttoned up -
Just whisper Catullus what she and you are up to.

56

I've got a funny one for you, Cato.
Lend me your ears and get ready to howl.
The more you love Catullus, Cato,
The more you'll laugh. It *is* funny.
In fact it's the joke of all jokes.

I surprised a lad bent on shafting his girl
And promptly rammed home my advantage.
Grateful thanks to the mother of Venus,
I found myself tailor-made for the job.

57

Don't they make a pretty pair?
If you fancy filthy sods.
Mamurra mirrors Caesar
(Arsehole elevation).
Why not? Their poxes match.
C. caught hers in Rome;
M. ditto in Formiae.
Tarred with the same brush, they are:
The kind that doesn't wash off.
Sick, sick, heavenly twins
In a single crib, tossing off
Mutual masterpieces.
Photofinish philanderers,
Dead heating for girls,
They'll come in a flash for your wife.
Don't they make a pretty pair?
If you fancy filthy sods.

58 a

Caelius, my Lesbia and yours, Lesbia the great,
The great Lesbia, the very one Catullus loved
More than himself and all he ever had,
Now all roads lead to her, the city's bottleneck,
Deepthroat for suckers from Rome's noblest stem.

58 b

If I was that Cretan automaton,
If I had wings like Pegasus,
If I was Ladas or wingfoot Perseus,
If I was Rhesus' fast, white pair -
If I was every fleetfoot feathered fowl
That ever flew, and wind to waft them,
I'd still give up, Camerius:
Give me any head start you like,
I'd still be drooping, weary to the bone,
Run down, gnawed by dumb fatigue.
Looking for *you*, chum, looking for *you*.

59

Rufa's a cocksucker, Rufulus her meat
A la Bolognese (yes, she's Menenius' wife);
Spot her on the beat most days
Around the necropolis, scoffing baked meats
Off the funeral pyres, juggling
Hot crusts as they tumble off the flames,
And getting her kicks from the Crematorium Operative
(Who doesn't even shave for the job).

60

Did a lioness spawn you in the mountains of death,
Or Scylla bark you out from her bitch's womb,
That you can be so cruel, so cynical,
Sniffing at my rawest, pitiful pain
With heart more savage than a beast's?
Numb, I ask you - hoping for the answer no.

61

Guardian of Helicon, Urania's son,
Come down: carry the gentle bride
Off to her husband. *O Hymen,*
    Hymenaeus, come!
Garland your hair with marjoram,
Soft-scented; veil your face and come
Smiling down to us, saffron shoes
    On milk-white feet.
Awakened on this happy day,
Join us in lusty marriage-songs,
Join us in dancing, holding high
    The marriage-torch.
For Junia comes to Manlius
As Venus of Idalium
Came to Paris, a lovely girl
    Blessed by the gods,
Lovely as flower-laden myrtle,
The toy of forest-nymphs, each branch
Their special care, tipped with blossom
    And wet with dew.
O Hymen, come! Come down to us
From the rocky slopes of Helicon
Where Aganippe's streams
    Run purling down.
Call the new mistress to her home,
Eager for her husband; twine her heart
Close with love, as ivy twines
    Close to the tree.

Bridesmaids-in-waiting, gather now
And lift harmonious voices
In the wedding-song: *O Hymen,*
    Hymen, Hymenaeus O!
Call his name, and summon him down

To bless this wedding-day: Hymen
Forerunner of Venus, lord
    Of the wedding-night.
You are the only lord of lovers:
Which other god can men prefer
Before you, lord? *O Hymen,*
    Hymen, Hymenaeus O!
The nervous father waits for you,
The bride, laying her girlhood down,
The eager groom, his ears alert
    For your footstep.
You will pluck the bride like a flower
From her mother's arms, and lay her
In his proud young arms. *O Hymen,*
    Hymen, Hymenaeus O!
Without your aid, there is no love
To leaven the wedding ritual
And give increase. Which of the gods
    Can equal you?
Without your aid, the house is bare
Of children; parents are barren
Without your aid. Which of the gods
    Can equal you?
Without your aid, the land lies bare
Of sons to guard it: only you
Can give it strength. Which of the gods
    Can equal you?

Open the doors; the bride is here.
See how the wedding-torches shake
Their heads, their fiery locks flying free
    To welcome her?
A shy young bride, half bashful
Half excited; she hesitates
Until love's calling draws her on
    Melting in tears.

No tears today! No girl on earth
So beautiful; no girl will see
A fairer wedding-day than this
    Dawn in the east.
Like you, the hyacinth, apart
From every flower in a rich man's
Pleasure garden: no more delay,
    The day is waiting.
Come forward, sweet, and hear our song;
Our torches dip their golden heads
To welcome you. This day is yours -
    Come forward, sweet.
No other woman's bed will lure
Your husband, no furtive lusts will draw
Him away from his soft repose
    Between your breasts,
But like the tree trunk gathered close
By the soft embracing vine,
So he in you. This day is yours -
    Come forward, sweet.
The marriage-couch, its polished legs,
Your lord's delight at hot mid-day
Or in the fleeting night; this day
    Is yours - come, sweet.
Lift high the torches: let them blaze
Bright as the wedding-veil. Come, sing
The wedding song. *O Hymen,*
    Hymen, Hymenaeus O!

Time for the age-old wedding jokes.
Hey, master's favourite, lonely now,
Your lord's love lost? Throw down the nuts,
    Nuts for the children.
Hey, limp little master's favourite,
Throw down nuts for the children. Not
For you, this time, the scramble for nuts:

Those games are done.
Yesterday you turned up your nose
At the greasy enticements of girls
From the fens; now you're shaving,
     Those days are done.
Does your master still hanker
After sleek, unshaven cheeks? No more:
Those days are done. *O Hymen,*
     Hymen, Hymenaeus O!
We know the sort of games you played,
The only ones: but married men
May not indulge. *O Hymen,*
     Hymen, Hymenaeus O!
His games now lie in his lady.
Lady, let him play how he will
Or he'll go roving. *O Hymen,*
     Hymen, Hymenaeus O!
You have wed into a house of power:
Blessed of your husband, take care
To keep it so. *O Hymen,*
     Hymen, Hymenaeus O!
Keep it just so, till grey old age,
Trembling, nods senile agreement
To every request.*O Hymen,*
     Hymen, Hymenaeus O!

With golden steps, lady, beloved
Of the gods, step forward, cross
The polished threshold. *O Hymen,*
     Hymen, Hymenaeus O!
Your lord waits on a royal couch
(Peep in and see): waits, rising
To welcome you. *O Hymen,*
     Hymen, Hymenaeus O!
His heart is on fire with love,
As yours is: his passion burns

Inside, deep down. *O Hymen,*
　　Hymen, Hymenaeus O!
Page-boy, let go her arm, her soft
Bride's arm; now she must go alone
To her husband's bed. *O Hymen,*
　　Hymen, Hymenaeus O!
Ladies-of-honour, worthy wives
Of worthy husbands, old in love,
Escort her in. *O Hymen,*
　　Hymen, Hymenaeus O!
Come now, husband; your wife waits
Pale as a white convolvulus
In the marriage-bed. *O Hymen,*
　　Hymen, Hymenaeus O!
Come, handsome youth, as blessed as she
With loveliness: come forward now.
Venus is with you: forward now,
　　The day is dying.
Come in, come in! Your love is there
For all to see. Venus is with you,
Desire in you made manifest.
　　No hiding now.
Far easier to count each grain of sand
In Africa, or tally the bright stars,
Than reckon up the games of love
　　You two will play.
Play on! Love's games make children,
Children an ancient line as proud
As yours demands. Play on, and sow
　　The future's seed.
Soon may a baby Manlius
Reach out soft hands from his mother's breast,
Laugh at his father, baby lips
　　Parted in joy.
May he grow so like his father
That all strangers acknowledge him

Noble as Manlius, modest
        As Manlius' wife,
The son honoured in his mother
As one other only, the son
Of Penelope flower of wives,
        Telemachus.

Girls, close the doors now. Our part
Is over. And you, happy pair,
God bless you. Practise your nimble youth
        In the gods' undying gift.

62

Up, boys: gather round. The evening star
Has tiptoed from heaven with lovely light.
Up, now: leave the fat feast. Hurry! The bride
Is coming: the songs will soon begin.
Hymen O Hymenaeus, Hymen Hymenaeus O!

    Up, girls: gather round. The boys are stirring,
    The night stars' evening lanterns lit.
    Look at the eager boys - eager to sing
    As we are eager to hear their song.
    Hymen O Hymenaeus, Hymen Hymenaeus O!

Now, boys: no easy task to win the contest -
The girls are practised, properly prepared,
With every note, every line, planted deep
In retentive minds, rehearsed with care.
Our ears, our minds, have often wandered, and
Victory (who favours careful preparation)
May not be ours. So listen now, at least.
Theirs to begin, and ours to answer them.
Hymen O Hymenaeus, Hymen Hymenaeus O!

O Hesperus, star of evening, cruellest
Of stars, you snatch from her mother's arms
The tender bride, snatch from her mother's arms
And hand to lusty groom his virgin bride -
No crueller fate when captured cities die!
Hymen O Hymenaeus, Hymen Hymenaeus O!

O Hesperus, star of evening, joyfullest
Of stars, you shine on the marriage-contract signed
And sealed long months before: at your bright glance
The dusty contract stirs, and comes to life -
No greater gift from heaven, no happier hour.
Hymen O Hymenaeus, Hymen Hymenaeus O!

Thief-Hesperus, who stole the girl away,
The loveliest of flowers, the thornless rose;
Thief-Hesperus, the lord of darkness, prince
Of thieves, your sly bright face appears, and says,
'Go out and steal! The secret night is now!'
Hymen O Hymenaeus, Hymen Hymenaeus O!

Thief-catcher Hesperus, when you arise
Night-watchmen see your light, and go to work.
Thieves hide, for Evening Star brings Morning light.
Girls call you thief, but in their hearts they say,
'Thief-Hesperus, come down and steal from me!'
Hymen O Hymenaeus, Hymen Hymenaeus O!

Like a flower cherished in a secret garden,
Safe from nibbling goat and rending plough,
Cradled by breezes, fed by sun and rain,
The delight of every boy and girl alike -
Then picked, stalk torn by a thin, sharp nail,
Torn and worthless, no one's darling now -
So now this girl: unblemished beauty then,
Beloved of all; but once your beauty's flower

Is plucked, who'll find in you their sweet delight?
Hymen O Hymenaeus, Hymen Hymenaeus O!

Like a vine, alone in a naked field;
Never erect, cradling no soft grapes;
Feeble body drooping, languid; twisted
Roots turning in to grasp their own shoots;
Unvisited by farmer or careful ox -
Then married at last to a sturdy elm,
And cherished by farmer and careful ox -
So now this girl: unfruitful spinster once,
Ageing and wan; but now your wedding-day
Has come, your husband's and parents' sweet delight.

Come then, sweet: come to this man, your
husband,
The husband chosen for you by your own father
And mother - your parents' choice. Obey them!
A virgin girl is only one third her own:
One third is her husband's, one her father's -
When two out of three unite, the third must
yield.
Your father paid his share: now you pay yours.
Hymen O Hymenaeus, Hymen Hymenaeus O!

63

The ship skims over deep water.
Eager feet jump down on Phrygian soil,
Hurry through trees to the goddess' sanctuary.
Mind awry, body stiff with frenzy . . .
Sharp flint . . . balls hanging heavy . . .
The cut. Unmanned now, mere man alone,
Blood spurting red spots on brown earth;

White hands snatch up the drum
(Cybele's drum, the Mother-mystery);
Soft fingers beat hollow hide;
His voice, trembling, chants to the others,
'This way! Dance to Cybele's grove,
This way, lost sheep of our lady of Dindymus!
You came like exiles to a strange land,
You braved salt currents, roaring seas,
You cut yourselves, not for Venus' love -
Dance faster, dance for your mistress!
No lagging - follow me further
To Cybele's secret, shaggy wood
Where cymbals clash, drums pound,
Curved reeds blow slow deep songs
And Maenads toss ivied heads,
Shrill voices hymning their sacred virginity -
Come where the goddess' flock wanders, fleet-foot;
Follow me; dance there, ever faster!'

So Attis, unman singing unsongs
To sudden, mindless Maenad-shrieks,
Bellowing drums and cymbals clashing,
Leads his unruly rout to Ida's green slopes.
Panting, frenzied, gasping for breath, lurching
To his own drum-beat through shadowy trees
Like a wild heifer bucking against the yoke.
The eunuch-priests race at his heels;
They reach Cybele's shrine, collapse
Exhausted, fasting, tumbled into sleep.

In the quiet night, the frenzy left their hearts.

But then the golden-visaged Sun 'gan rise,
And swept the sky, the land, the sea with eyes
Of flashing fire; his chargers put to flight
With clattering hooves the shadows of the night.

Then Sleep took fright, and, leaving Attis, fled
With haste to join his eager wife, in bed.
So, out of gentle rest, all passion spent,
Young Attis woke. His eyes he downward bent,
And clear-eyed, saw what his own hands had wrought,
Saw what he lacked, and how things were, and thought.
His heart awash with cares, he made his way
Back to the shore, and gazed (as well he may)
Far out across the vasty deep, his eyes
Abrim with tears. He thinks of home, and cries:

'O Greece, who sowed me; Greece, who bore me;
Greece, whom I left, as errant slaves
Desert their masters; I came to Ida
Where wild beasts shiver in snowy lairs;
I came to visit their savage mountain lairs -
O Greece, where are you now?
My eyes seek you out, eagerly, in brief
Hours of lucidity. Why, oh why
Did I leave you for this nothingness?
My home, my wealth, my friends, my parents,
Market-place, school, stadium, gymnasium -
Break, my heart, break for bitterness.
Men loved me once, whatever form I chose:
I was woman, young man, beardless youth and boy,
Flower of the gym, pride of the changing-room;
My doorstep was crowded, my threshold warm;
When the sun awoke, and I left my bed,
My entrance was always hung around with flowers.
And now I must be a nun, Cybele's slave,
A Maenad, half my own true self, a human mule.
My home must be Ida, shivering under snow,
By the honeycomb hermit-caves of Phrygia,
Sharing the forest-glades of deer and boar.
If only I . . . If only . . .'

His rosy lips gave forth this bitter cry,
Unwelcome sounds, that reached the gods on high.
Cybele heard, and hearing, loosed the yoke
That held her lion, spurred him on, and spoke:
'Go forth, my strong one, drive him mad again;
Make him return to me, distraught, insane -
This foolish boy who longs to leave my shores.
Go: lash your tail, and utter fearful roars
Till all the woods and hills for miles resound.'
Thus spoke fierce Cybele, and with one bound
Her lion went forth to do her will. He leapt
From rock to rock, as down the path he swept;
He lashed his tail; he growled; he roared; his wrath
Broke down the very thickets in his path.
At last he finds the sea-washed shore, and spies
The gentle Attis there, all torn with sighs.
He roars, and charges. Like a startled deer
The lovely boy takes flight. The woods are near
And he escapes; but now, for evermore,
He lives, Cybele's slave, in durance sore.

O goddess, great goddess, Cybele, lady of Dindymus,
O lady, send no frenzy on my house.
Keep it for others, lady: send others mad.

64

In days of yore (they say) when pines could skim
Through Neptune's crystal kingdom, some did swim
To Phasis' waters, lord Aeëtes' land.
These pines (Mount Pelion's children) bore a band
Of noble youths - the heart and flower of Greece -
To Colchis, there to steal the Golden Fleece.
On sailed th' intrepid band, with graceful ease

75

Sweeping (and firwood oars) the darkling seas.
Athene - lady of citadels - her aid
Had lent, meshed pines together, *Argo* made.
She taught the unskilled bark its lofty prow
Through Amphitrite's stormy realm to plough.
The water (churned by oars to foam) turned white;
The sea-nymphs raised their heads to see the sight,
And wonder as the monster passed them by.
The sailors too looked out with mortal eye
To see (once only) sea-nymphs swimming there
With proud upstanding breasts, their bodies bare
Against the whitening spume. Then Peleus saw
Fair Thetis; Thetis (filled with equal awe)
Her Peleus spied, and loved. Lord Neptune said,
'So be it! Mortal and immortal, wed!'

O heroes, born in such propitious times,
Offspring of gods, good mothers' sons, my lines
Salute you, now and evermore: I greet
You every one! All honours at your feet
Especially, proud Peleus, prop and stay
Of Thessaly! Great Jove himself gave way
And yielded his love to you. Fair Thetis came
And married you, the crown of nymphs. Your fame
Won you marriage with Tethys' grand-daughter,
And old Oceanus' (grandsire of water).

No more waiting now: the day has come at last.
The palace bulges with guests: all Thessaly
Is here, filling the courts with joy and excitement.
Each visitor brings his wedding-gift; each face
Glows with pleasure. They have come from Cieros,
Thessalian Tempe, even from distant Crannon
And the castles of Larissa. Pharsalus is crammed tight:
Every house is full. Only the fields lie empty;
The bullocks' necks are soft with ease; the vines

Huddle in tight rows, fighting unhoed weeds.
No oxen are ploughing, no sickles thin the leaves;
Farm-implements lie rusting in the fields.

Every corner of the palace glitters with gold and silver,
Thrones inlaid with ivory, cups glinting on the tables;
Treasure piled high reflects the joy of festival.
In the centre stands the goddess' throne,
Polished ivory, with a proud purple coverlet,
A superb historical tapestry
Embroidered with uncanny skill,
Showing the deeds of the heroes of the past.
On this side, look! Ariadne stands on Naxos
Looking out to sea, as Theseus sails away.
The poor girl is half-demented:
She can't believe her eyes; it's as though
She's just woken up from a nightmare,
Only to find herself on a deserted beach.
Theseus has forgotten her; bending to the oars
He hurries away, scattering promises to the winds.
Ariadne stands there on the seaweed
Looking after him with tear-filled eyes,
Like a Bacchant carved in stone.
The tides of her misery ebb and flow
Like the sea itself. Her fair hair is loose,
Not covered with the usual fine-spun scarf;
The clothes have fallen unheeded from her body,
The filmy dress, the woven cord
That supports her milky breasts; all lie
Forgotten at her feet, washed by the salty sea.
Her thoughts are not on scarves or dresses:
Her whole heart, her whole tortured mind,
Her whole being is fixed on Theseus.
Poor soul! Venus drove her mad
And sowed cares in her heart like thorns,
Beginning when Theseus the Bold set sail

From the curved coastline of Piraeus
On his way to Crete and the barbarian tyrant's throne.

They say that it all began with a cruel plague
That forced the Athenians to pay the price
For killing Androgeos; and every year they picked
The choicest boys, the ripest girls, as food
For the Cretan Minotaur. Athens was small,
And the loss each year was grievous.
So Theseus, on behalf of the people he loved,
Chose himself as voluntary sacrifice,
To make this cargo of living dead the last
To sail from Athens to cruel Crete.
So, sail spread and the wind behind him,
He came to mighty Minos and his proud palace.

As soon as princess Ariadne saw him
He dazzled her; she was a pure bloom,
Tended by loving mother in virgin bed,
Like the myrtle-trees of Eurotas
Or bright flowers tempted out by a light spring breeze.
Her eyes burned with Theseus; the fire
Licked through her whole body,
Consuming her very marrow with thoughts of him.
O Cupid! What passions you awaken,
Joy and care mixed in the same cup!
And you, Venus, lady of Golgi and leafy Idalium,
The girl is afire, and you torment her
With tides of passion, languishing sighs
Of love for her fair, blond visitor -
Love, and fear in her fainting heart.
She turned paler than gold
To see Theseus' passion to fight
The Minotaur (death or eternal fame the prize).
Her prayers rose to the gods above,
Muttered prayers, half-uttered promises.

The gods heard: for just as in the Taurus hills
Oak trees, or resin-oozing conifers
Are snatched by a greedy whirlwind,
Torn up and die, twisted roots
Dislocated, toppling everything in their path -
So Theseus felled the mighty Minotaur
As it tossed its horns vainly to the vaunting winds.
Then, carefully, clutching his triumph to him,
He threaded his way back along the line
Of life, laid thinly through the corridors
In case the Labyrinth amazed him.

So far: and I digress. What more?
Shall I tell how she turned from her father's face,
The embrace of her sister and her mother
(Leaving her weeping for a daughter lost) -
Turned from them, for Theseus' sweet love's sake?
Shall I tell of her voyage to booming Naxos,
Or how, when her eyes were locked in sleep,
Her Theseus crept away, his heart set
On other things? She wept (the story goes);
Madness flickered and sputtered in her breast;
Weeping, she climbed the frowning cliffs
To gaze out over the empty, endless sea.
Then down, fast, into the water,
(Lifting her clothes, thighs bare),
And spoke these sad words, this last complaint,
Sobs pouring from foam-flecked lips:

'Theseus! Traitor! You tore me
From my father's altars, and left me
Here on this deserted shore! Forgetting your duty,
You sailed for home - your cargo a full hold
Of treachery. Could nothing stop you?
Had you no mercy, no pity left for me?
This ending was not the one you promised

(Soft words honeying my eager ears):
You promised marriage, and my heart leapt.
Marriage! A promise written on the wind!
From now on let all women learn from me:
No man who swears will ever keep his word.
So long as they want something from you,
Want it desperately, they promise worlds;
But once their desire is satisfied
They go, and do not call it treachery.
O Theseus! You were caught
In the whirlwind of death, and I saved you.
I killed my Minotaur-brother for you,
And you deserted me. Food for carrion birds
Is what I am: unburied, unentombed.
What lioness bore you, alone
In a lonely cave? What sea engendered you,
To spit you out from its frothing waves
On Crete? What Scylla, what Charybdis
Nursed you, taught you these thanks?
O Theseus! If you never intended marriage
(Because of strict orders from your father?)
You could still have taken me home
Your slave, your happy slave,
Happy to wash your white feet
And spread a purple cover on your bed.
Who hears my misery? The dull winds?
They see me driven mad, and pass by
Unheeding, careless, deaf and dumb.
O Theseus! Where are you? Far out to sea
And well on the way to Athens? No man stirs
On this empty sand; I am alone;
Not even the cruel Fates hear my grief.
O Jupiter, if only those Athenian ships
Had never made landfall in Crete!
If only that traitor had never come
To anchor, with his cruel cargo, his cruel

80

Deception masked by a handsome face!
This evil nestling, roosting in my heart!

'Where shall I turn to next? Go home?
The rough sea lies between us. Turn
To my father? The father I left to chase
A cruel Athenian, spattered with my brother's blood?
A husband, then? A faithful husband
To cherish my misery away? He is gone,
His oars bending to beat the sullen sea!
Naxos is empty: no houses, no escape,
Nothing but endless sea.
No escape, no hope, no human voice
To comfort me; death on every side.
Death? No! I shall not die
Until I show my loyalty to heaven,
And beg their loyalty in answer.
O Furies, who live to bring pain
To criminals, whose hair stands stiff with snakes,
Whose faces freeze with your hearts' fierce anger;
O Furies, come! Listen to me now,
As I weep my frustration to the barren sand,
Love-blackened, blind with mindless grief.
My misery is plain: it comes
From deep in my heart. Accept it, then,
Grim goddesses! Take Theseus, as heedless now
As when he left me - help him kill
Himself, grim Furies, himself and all his line!'

So Ariadne: sad words, and a sad heart.
The ruler of the gods heard,
And nodded approval. At his nod
The sky and bristling sea shuddered,
And earth crashed against the sky.
But Theseus, his mind blurred with mist,
His heart empty, forgot his orders,

The orders fixed securely till now.
Long before, when Aegeus of Athens
Gave his dear son to the winds, for Crete,
He embraced the young man and said,
'O my dear boy, dearer to me than life,
My son, restored to me at my long life's end,
Since both my fate and your fiery spirit
Are snatching you away before my tired eyes
Have feasted their fill of your dear shape,
I will not send you off with a light heart
Or give you good omens for comfort -
Not till I pour out my complaints,
Strewing my grey hair with ash and dust
And hanging dark sails to your masthead -
Dark-dyed sails to show our grief
And the misery burning in our hearts.
Then, if our lady Athene (who guides
Our nation, the people of Erechtheus)
Allows you to bathe your hands in that bull's blood
And win, remember these instructions
(Store them carefully, for time can blur them):
As soon as you see Athenian hills again,
Take down the dark-dyed sails from the masthead
And rope up new white sails
That will catch my eye, and warm my heart
With joy at your safe return.'

These were his father's orders. Theseus
Had remembered them till now; but now, as clouds
Drift on the winds' breath from snowy mountain-peaks,
They left him.
His father, on the high tower straining out
To sea, saw dark sails. A river of lamentation
Flooded his eyes, and he threw himself down
On the rocks below, thinking his Theseus dead.
So Theseus the Bold returned to a house of grief:

His own heart knew the same pain
His treachery had brought forgotten Ariadne.

And Ariadne stood on the beach in Naxos, her mind
Seething with sad anxiety. Then, further down,
The coverlet showed another scene: Bountiful Bacchus
Leaping along with his Satyr-train
Looking for Ariadne, hot for her love.
His Bacchants ran behind him, nimbly,
Wits wandering, heads tossing
To the Evoe-chant, thyrsuses shaking.
Some played catch with the torn limbs
Of a ripped-up bullock; others wore
Hissing snakes for garlands;
Others bore secret, sacred objects
(Baskets for secrecy, hidden from uninitiates);
Others beat drums with soft white fingers
Or tinkled tiny cymbals; others yet blew horns
Or whistled tunes on piercing, foreign flutes.

These are the scenes embroidered on the coverlet,
Magnificent, unique to Thetis' holy couch,
Unique in the wide world. The young people
Of Thessaly crowd round to see - then draw back
Respectfully, making way for the holy gods.
It is like the breeze rippling the marble sea,
The morning breeze, teasing the waves to tips
As Dawn arises, leaving the wandering Sun.
At first the breeze is gentle, the waves quiet,
A ripple, a chuckle of water;
But soon the winds freshen, the wave-tips
Glint in the rising sun, running races over the wide sea.
So Peleus' guests as they left, each for his home.

The mortals gone, the gods came calling. First, Chiron
From the slopes of Pelion. His gifts, trees and shrubs:

All the produce of Thessaly, the fruit of the high hills,
River-flowers warmed by soft west winds,
Garlands, nosegays of laughter and honey-scents.
Next, Peneus the river-god, and Tempe
Shaggy with trees, where Dorian revellers dance.
Their gifts: tall beech-trees, roots and all;
High, slender laurels; plane-trees too,
The supple sisters of fiery Phaethon; poplars
Whose tips touch heaven. All these they weave
In a broad screen, a murmurous canopy
Of soft green leaves.
Next, wily Prometheus (the scars of his chains still livid,
Slow to fade). Then Jupiter himself, king of heaven,
With his queen and children attending. Only Phoebus
Is left in the sky, and Artemis, home in the hills
Of Idrias: Artemis and Phoebus her brother
Scorn Peleus, and stay away from the wedding.

When the gods are seated (on snow-white thrones
Of polished ivory, beside rich-laden tables),
The aged Fates appear, to chant the future.
Their shaking limbs are clothed in the white robes
Of old age, purple-bordered at the ankle;
Their hair, like twisting snow on their aged heads,
Is garlanded with roses. As they sing, they spin:
Their left hands hold the distaffs, clothed
In soft wool; their right hands, carefully,
Draw off the threads into their upturned fingers,
Then deftly turn it back, and run
The whirling spindle on its rounded wheel.
And as they work the wool, their teeth tease
The threads smooth, tugging out rough particles.
Shreds of wool fleck their withered lips,
But the woven thread is smooth and clear.
At their feet, wicker baskets fill
With balls of soft, white thread.

84

And as they spin, in clear voices
They sing a sacred song, a song of the future,
Binding, irrevocable,
A song to outlast every age to come:

'O Peleus, prop of Emathia, the pride
And joy of Jupiter, the glorious, the strong,
Hear what we sing to you, a holy song,
Our prophecy to you and your immortal bride.
    *Spindles, run on, run on, draw out the fine-spun
    thread.*
Lord Hesperus will come, the evening star,
Bearing rich gifts; your lady Thetis, too,
Your bride, will come, longing to lie with you
In easeful sleep, from care and sorrow far.
    *Spindles, run on, run on, draw out the fine-spun
    thread.*
No house has seen a love like yours before;
No bond so binding, none by heaven's eyes
So gladly witnessed. Who would dare surmise
If she loves you, or you love her, the more?
    *Spindles, run on, run on, draw out the fine-spun
    thread.*
Your son will be Achilles, foe to fear;
His back to enemies a stranger, not his face;
A runner too, the best in any race,
Who step for step will match the fastest deer.
    *Spindles, run on, run on, draw out the fine-spun
    thread.*
Achilles! On every battlefield his face
Will rout the enemy; when Trojan blood
Pours over the Phrygian plains in scarlet flood
Lord Agamemnon will yield the leader's place.
    *Spindles, run on, run on, draw out the fine-spun
    thread.*
At funerals, when aged mothers beat

Their shrivelled breasts with shaking hands, and tear
For pity's sake each straggling, greying hair,
Their sons they'll mourn, Achilles' fame repeat.
   *Spindles, run on, run on, draw out the fine-spun
   thread.*
Just as a reaper cuts the swathes of grain
In summer, when the ripened ears hang low,
So will the Trojans fall, with every blow
Achilles' sword win ever greater fame.
   *Spindles, run on, run on, draw out the fine-spun
   thread.*
Scamander's mighty flow will speak his name
As down it runs towards the foaming sea;
Its waters narrowed, choked, not running free,
Filled to the depths with bodies of the slain.
   *Spindles, run on, run on, draw out the fine-spun
   thread.*
Polyxena, the girl they give to Death
(Her snow-white limbs laid on his funeral-pyre,
A sacrifice in lord Achilles' fire)
Will witness to his name with her last breath.
   *Spindles, run on, run on, draw out the fine-spun
   thread.*
For then, when Troy succumbs to Greek attacks,
Poseidon's locks give way, the city dies,
The girl will fall for him, her piteous cries
Cut in her throat by sacrificial axe.
   *Spindles, run on, run on, draw out the fine-spun
   thread.*
So hurry, Peleus, take your heavenly bride;
And Thetis, go to meet your mortal groom:
Love and enjoyment fill the marriage-room
And blessings shower the royal pair inside.
   *Spindles, run on, run on, draw out the fine-spun
   thread.*
Her nurse, returning with the sun's first light,

Must find a married woman, not a girl, inside;
Her mother, anxious for the virgin bride,
No quarrel find, but hopes of children bright.
  *Spindles, run on, run on, draw out the fine-spun
  thread.'*

These future joys the Fates told Peleus,
Speaking the thoughts of their prophetic hearts.
For in those distant days the gods
Were not ashamed to visit, and be seen,
In the houses of mortal men.
Often, Jupiter himself came out
At festival-time from his gleaming temple,
To watch priests sacrifice the hecatomb.
Or Bacchus, wandering the peaks of Parnassus,
Drove the Bacchants before him, hair streaming,
While the people of Delphi welcomed him with
    smoking altar-fires.
In war, too, in struggles to the death, Mars himself,
Or the lady of Triton, or Nemesis of Rhamnus,
Appeared in person, urging on the combatants.

Those days are past. Now,
When the earth is choked with greed, injustice, crime -
When brothers soak their hands in brothers' blood,
Or children laugh to see their parents die,
When a father prays for the death of his son
So that he can marry a virgin daughter-in-law,
Or a mother comes gasping beneath her own son's lust -
Careless of our common, divine ancestry,
We have totally confused good and evil
And the gods have turned their faces from us.
No one sees a god face to face today,
Face to face in the clear light of day.

65

Exhausted with grief, Hortalus, drawn by care
From serving the learned Nine, my mind,
Storm-tossed on a sea of misery, cannot
Now bear the Muses' lovely children,
Barren since the day when in Lethe's swamps
Insistent water lapped his bloodless feet -
My brother, snatched away by fate, buried
In Trojan earth beside the Hellespont.
O dear brother, dearer than my life,
Shall I never see you more? No more:
You are gone. But my love still lives,
In sad verses singing your death
As Procne sings, in dark Daulian trees,
For her dear son Itylus, the son she killed.
Exhausted as I am with grief, Hortalus,
I send a poem of Callimachus
Translated to please you (for you must not think
Your words forgotten, written on the wind) -
A small token that slipped from my care
Like an apple, sent as a sign of love
To a pretty girl: innocent, she hides it
In her bosom, under her dress, and forgets it;
Then up she jumps for her mother, the apple
Tumbles to the floor, and a guilty blush
Crimsons her face, an apple of dismay.

66

The observer of every star in the wide sky, whose
  charts
Show their rising and their setting,
The darkening of the sun's bright fire,
The waning of each constellation
And the moon's sweet, stolen love-trips from the sky
To the rocky caves of Latmos;
Conon, the royal astronomer, observer of all this,
Saw me, too, on the sky-threshold:
A lock of queen Berenice's golden hair, offered
To tempt every goddess in heaven
When her husband (rich in his marriage, and fresh
From the triumph of the wedding-night -
His maiden bride the spoils of battle) started out
To conquer Syria.

Do new brides hate love? Or are the tears they weep
Outside the marriage-room - tears
That destroy their parents' happiness - false tears?
Yes, false: compare them
With the genuine grief of my lady Berenice
As her husband left for war.
Was it your empty marriage-bed that grieved you, lady,
Or a genuine cause, your husband's death?
The pain was deep: it gnawed your heart, left you
Fainting, miserable, torn with sobs.
You became a timid girl again, afraid to remember
The deed that proved you strong -

Having assassinated her first husband Demetrius (for adultery with her
own mother) queen Berenice of Egypt married Ptolemy III. Soon after
the marriage he set out to attack Syria. Berenice promised to cut off a
lock of her hair if he returned safely. On his safe return, the hair was
placed in a temple, but mysteriously disappeared. Later, the royal
astronomer Conon identified a new constellation; to this day it is still
called 'Berenice's hair', Coma Berenices.

A noble deed: a royal assassination! - a deed no other
Dared, the deed that made you queen!
And such a girl as this - to weep such tears as these
For a husband, rub her eyes so red?
Which of the gods had power to change you? Can
    lovers
Not bear to be so long apart?
As your sweet husband left for the war, you offered me
To the powers above, with fearful oaths,
If he came safely back. Back he came, with Asia
Captive, added to Egypt's lands.
And for his success I am now a star - an ancient
    promise,
Fulfilled in a strange new way.

O lady, by your royal head I swear,
An oath that no one safely makes in vain,
I was snipped untimely from your head.
But which of us can argue with hard steel?
Mount Athos yielded (highest of all the lands
The bright Sun, Thia's offspring, travels over);
King Xerxes' steel created out of land
Another sea: the Persian host sailed through
The midst of Athos. And if might like that
Gives way to steel, what hope have locks of hair?
Great Jupiter, destroy those Chalybes,
Who first discovered veins of ore beneath
The ground, who first learned how to make cast iron!
My sister-locks had just begun to mourn
My fate, when all at once the West Wind came
(Brother of Ethiopian Memnon) swooping down
On beating wings; Arsinoe's wingéd steed,
He snatched me up, bore me away across
The shadowy sky to Venus' virgin breast -
That was his task, the guerdon on him laid
By his lady Arsinoe, the Locrian,

The Greek whose shrine by proud Canopus stands.
Then Venus - lest fair Ariadne's crown
Of gold should be the only mortal star
In the bright firmament, and wanting me
(The promised gift of golden hair) to shine
Beside it - took me up, still damp with spray
Collected on the ride from sea to sky,
And set me here: a new star mid the old.
On one side Virgo, on the other Leo,
And next to me Callisto, the Great Bear.
I sink to rest before the Waggoner
Boötes, who dips below the horizon
Just as each new day dawns. At night I lie
Full in the highway of the gods; the dawn
Restores me to white-haired Tethys. And still,
O Nemesis (if I may say so freely,
Speak what is in my heart, however much
The stars tear me to pieces afterwards),
However much I like my present state,
I still remember where I used to be,
On Berenice's head: remember, and weep.

While she was still a virgin girl, we two
A thousand lovely perfumes knew,
Before untried. So, young brides, seeing at last
The longed-for torches gleam,
Before you join body to body with your loving
    husbands
(Clothes thrown aside, breasts bare),
Remember to offer me up a gift of perfume -
A gift, that is, from those of you
Who give their marriage due honour: adulterers' gifts
Are foul, fit only for dust to drink.
I want no gifts from wicked girls. Stay faithful, brides,
Faithful and happy,
And may undying Love light on your marriages.

And you, lady Berenice:
'When you look up at the stars, in the torchlight
   sacrifice
To Venus, remember me:
I am your own - grant me a gift of perfume,
Poured lavishly, till every star
Cries out, 'If only I, too, were a lock of royal hair -
Forget how bright that bright Orion shines!'

67

Well, hi there, Door! A husband, a father
Should live so long, to get a door like you.
Took a real shine to Balbus, didn't you -
That old guy who used to own this place?
But Balbus Jnr, and that girl of his
When the old boy snuffed it: not your scene
At all. So what's with you, Door, all at once?
Why change? Why quit the loyal retainer bit?

Please, sir, not so loud: the new master may hear,
Master Caecilius. They say it was all my fault,
You know. *Most* unfair. They blame it all on me.
'If there's no one to pin it to, pin it on the door' -
That's their line, and I take it really hard.

Aw, come on, Door: there's more to it than that.
Out with it. Give. We wanna know the facts.

Who wants to know sir? Who wants to know the
   facts?

I *wanna know the goddam facts! So, give.*

92

Oh, very well, sir. First of all, you know
They say she was a virgin? I knew you'd laugh.
I mean, it's not as if he didn't *try* -
That poor young man never could get it up . . .
A sad, blunt instrument . . . no prick to it at all.
So the father . . . mmm, in his own son's bed . . .
Bringing shame and disgrace to the whole house . . .
Of course, we don't *know* it was simple, groping lust:
It may have been an honest attempt to *help* his son
(Poor flabby boy!) to plant a sturdy seed
In a maiden furrow. No, *cherchez l'homme*, I say.

Sure, Door, a father only doing his duty,
Getting it together to help his son.

Oh, that's not all, sir. Brixia knows a tale
Or two. You know, Brixia? 'Brixia, nestling close
To Cycnus' watchtower, Brixia softly washed
By yellow Mella's streams, Brixia beloved,
The mother-city of our own beloved Verona' . . .
Yes, *that* Brixia. She talks of *another* pair
Of lovers . . . Postumus . . . Cornelius . . . such
  goings-on!
Now, now, I know what you're going to say:
'How does a stick-in-the-rut door like you
Know that? You're fixed there under your lintel,
With nothing to do but open and shut all day.'
Well, I'm telling you I heard it from her *own* lips . . .
Often . . . gossiping with the maids . . . her
  life-story . . .
Naming names, even (the ones I mentioned) . . .
You'd think she didn't know I had a pair of ears
To hear, and a tongue to tell. *And* that's not all:
There was another lover. Shh! No names this time -
One frown from him, and I'd be firewood -
A long, lean man . . . there was a law-suit . . .
A long, lean suit . . . paternity . . . all lies, of
  course . . .   93

68

You sent me a tearful letter - I have it here:
Crushed by fortune . . . utterly distraught . . .
A shipwrecked sailor on a foam-washed beach . . .
Feet poised on the threshold of death . . .
You ask me to drag you back, to offer your heart
Some ease. *Venus torments me . . . I toss and turn . . .*
I'm alone, in a single bed . . . I try reading . . .
The old, sweet songs . . . the Muses will lull me
    asleep . . .
But they don't. You lay down the old songs,
And ask me for a new love-song, a friend's gift.

Dear Mallius, don't think me unsympathetic.
I understand - and I know the duty
Friend owes friend. But like you, I too
Am 'crushed by fortune'; *my* heart's 'awash with care'.
I spent the flowery spring of youth
In studying (beginning the day I came of age).
My subject: love. I learned every game
The laughing goddess plays, who mixes joy and care.
I was a good student, promised well -
Until he died, and stole my joy.
O dear brother, stolen away,
My life's light, I died, I went to the grave
With you; my happiness (kept alive alone
In loving you, alive) died with your death.
When you died I gave up my studies,
Withdrew from my courses, abandoned
All my researches into pleasure.

So when you write, *Things must be bad,*
Catullus, there in Verona: even here in Rome
The best people warm themselves - in a widow's
    bed . . .

Things aren't that bad in Verona,
Not bad like that at all.
You ask me for a friend's gift, Mallius.
Please understand, my grief gives me no gifts
To give. Here in Verona, I've no desk
Bulging with manuscripts: my desk -
My youth! - I left behind in Rome,
And here I live from a single trunk.
All this to explain why this time
I can't deliver the goods: no lack
Of affection, no shirking of obligations -
I simply can't supply
Goods (at the moment) not in stock.

And yet, I must speak out: I must tell
Every detail of Mallius' unstinting friendship.
Take up the story, Muses: even when
These sheets grow old, keep them alive -
Don't let the immemorial flight of time
Darken them into blind obscurity,
Or spiders weave lofty, insubstantial webs
Round Mallius' immortality.

When two-faced Venus had my heart in thrall,
Scorched through with passion, shaken and convulsed
With volcanic tides of love, that kept my eyes
Misty with weeping, my cheeks as dewed with tears
As a rivulet on a lofty mountain-side
That bubbles down from rock to mossy rock
(A stream that soon, tumbling to the valley floor,
Will make its way past stately poplar trees,
Refresh the traveller sweating on his way
And slake the parched fields' thirsty furrows):
Such was my state - as sailors lost at sea
In a crow-black storm cry out in desperate need
To Castor and Pollux for a gentler breeze -

Such was my state: my rescuer, Mallius.
He found us a private place, my love and me,
A secret house where we might safely love.
Then in she walked, my goddess, with steps as sure
As a virgin bride: worn doorstep, fair white feet . . .
I remember, her sandal squeaked (an omen).

Like Laodamia, when she first set foot
In doomed Protesilaus' house, hot with love,
In a union unsanctified by sacrifice
Or the pacific ceremonial of heaven.
(O lady Nemesis, may I never act
In such hot haste, without my lords' approval).
Later (husband lost) Laodamia learned
How the thirsty altar must drink holy blood
Before a bride submits to her lusty groom.
He went; she waited; winter came and went
And came again, filling her starving heart
With love unsatisfied, teaching her to live
Without her husband, snatched (as the Fates well knew)
For ever, that day he went to fight at Troy.

Troy! With Helen's rape as bait to draw
The leaders of Greece, a clarion-call to death;
Troy! Mass grave of Europe and Asia,
Bitter dust of heroes and heroic pride;
Troy! You stole my unhappy brother too,
Stole him away. O dear brother, stolen away,
My life's light, I died, I went to the grave
With you; my happiness (kept alive alone
In loving you, alive) died with your death.
You lie, not reverently in a familiar tomb
With those who loved you, but far away
In Troy, foul Troy, Troy at the end of the world,
That clawed you down to lie in foreign earth.

They flocked there then, the choice young men of
  Greece;
They left their hearths and homes, and flocked to
  Troy
To stop Paris taking his pleasure in Helen,
Unchallenged pleasure in a bed of ease.
And for this - for this! - fair Laodamia,
Your husband (dearer than life, than breath itself)
Was snatched away: your love and his, climbing
To climax in melting passion, was plunged
From the high peaks to the chilly depths - a pit
As deep, as fathomless, as Hercules once dug
(Hercules, Greek-named 'son of Amphitryon')
At Pheneus, at the foot of Mount Cyllene,
Dug to drain the marsh, and dry the fertile soil,
Dug through the very marrow of the mountain
As soon as the Stymphalian birds were dead,
Struck with unerring arrows, as his cruel lord
Had ordered: his obedience opened the gates
Of Olympus to him, won him Hebe's love.
That pit was deep; but deeper still the pit
Engulfing your lofty love, humbling your pride.
Your husband was dear to you, dearer far
Than a grandson born to an only daughter,
Born to warm an old man's feeble heart,
Born at last to inherit an old man's wealth,
To enter his name on the tablets of the will
(Stripping the joy from the circling next-of-kin
Who hover like vultures round the old man's head.)
White doves, they say, are loyal lovers,
Devoted lovers, snatching kisses
With impetuous, darting beaks, their love
A flame fiercer than in any woman's heart -
Fiercer than any flame but yours, Laodamia,
As you lapped your lovely lover then.

Like Laodamia, my Lesbia, then,
My shining passion, ran to my arms
While Cupid fluttered happily above,
Her smiling page-boy, dressed for a wedding.
And now, you say, Catullus is not enough
For her, she warms others in her widow's bed?
I must allow her a few indiscretions:
I'll not play the fool, the slave of jealousy.
Remember: Juno, queen of heaven, knew
Her flighty lord's multifarious affairs,
Knew them all, and choked her anger back.
No point in mortals outdoing the gods;
No point in playing the palsied cuckold -
She did not come to me on her father's arm
(To that house, smelling of Syrian musk!);
She came secretly, at night, and gave me
A priceless gift, stolen from her husband's lap.
No, I am satisfied: enough for me
If she counts *my* days red-letter days.

There, Mallius. A love-poem. A friend's gift,
My best return for generous help.
Your name will live for ever now, free of rust,
Today, tomorrow and tomorrow and tomorrow,
Let the gods grant as many tomorrows
As ever Justice granted the pure in heart.
God bless you, Mallius. Long life to you;
Long life to the house you lent us,
The ground and beginning of all our bliss.
Like a true friend, you gave me happiness:
My mistress, dearer to me than all the world,
My daylight, focus of all my life and love.

69

Stop asking, Rufus, why 'the girls'
Won't 'tender you their downy thighs',
Why Dior dresses cut no ice,
Or transparent jewels with clear designs.
Rank rumour's cut you down to size:
'His armpits shelter goats - in flocks'.
That's why 'the girls' don't fancy you:
What nice young thing would warm to *that*?
So - Stamp Out Nasal Torture Now,
Or don't ask why the girls turn tail.

70

No man, she insists, she'd marry before me,
Not if Jupiter himself were cap in hand.
Insists? What women say to men in love
Are scribbles on water, whispers in the wind.

71

Two personal problems: under-arm goat
And athlete's feet - your gifts to a rival
Who tried to saddle up your mount.
It serves him right, the greedy sod:
Now, when he fucks, you pay them both -
She gets the goat; he ends up limp.

72

Once upon a time, it was only Catullus,
Lesbia: you'd have turned down Jove in his place.
I loved you - not as any Jack loves Jill:
Whole families get less than I gave you.
But now I know you better - and the brand
Burns even deeper. How is that? Don't I know
You're vile, you're cheap? *Because* I know. Because.
The more you love a bitch, the more you're bound to
    hate.

73

Forget gratitude, from anyone, for anything.
Earn their respect, you think? Do good?
No good. The world's all graceless now.
Smile, and they yawn you out of their way.
Take me: who hurts me most, and salts the wound?
A man who called me once 'My one and only friend'.

74

Friend Gellius was warned: 'Uncle's a stickler,
One of the old school - no smut, clean mouth, clean
    hands.'
And Gellius didn't want trouble. He made his play
For Auntie, and dealt Uncle a hand as well.
First wish, then deed. What? Silence from Uncle?
The old school doesn't talk with its mouth full.

75

Launched in madness then, Lesbia, am I. Your fault.
And mine, wrecked by my own fidelity, the fool.
Worthless, though you turn saint;
Unforgettable, whatever you do.

76

Can the heart ever recover yesterday's delight,
When a man knows that he did well and right,
Never broke his solemn word, nor said 'By god, I will,'
And then did not, nor men or gods served ill?
Many then the joys, Catullus, that remain
To cheer your life, from this love's graceless pain.
For whatever men well say or well can do,
That has been said, that has been done by you.
Done and said in vain: squandered on a spendthrift
    heart.
Why twist again the rack that racks you apart?
Stop, stop. Be firm, Catullus. Enough of this vile mess.
The gods say 'no'; damn what they will not bless.
It's difficult to shed so quick so long a love?
It *is* difficult. Ways can and must be thought of.
One hope you have: conquer yourself, the game is won.
Possible? Not possible? It must be done.
Oh gods, call up your pity, shown to men before,
That last reprieve, arrived at Death's open door;
See how it is with me and, for your pity's sake,
Tear from my soul this pestilence, this snake,
That does my inmost being coil and paralyse
And to my heart all happiness denies.
My old prayer I pray no longer: that her cold heart
    relent

Or that - by chance - she play the penitent.
To be whole, oh gods, I pray, and of this madness
    free;
For pity's sake, restore my sanity.

77

To Rufus

The red-handed.
    In vain I trusted you, and for nothing, friend.
For nothing?
    When I've paid and paid and paid?
So and so,
    Creep, name branded on my heart.
Thief,
    Who took from me all that I found good.
Misery.
    It hurts, it hurts. Arsenic of my life.
It hurts,
    It hurts, rat that called yourself my friend.

78 a

Gallus had brothers; one with a dishy wife,
    The other with a dish for a son.
Gallus is a sweetie, and sweet on sweethearts;
    The lovely lad he peddles to the lovely lass.
Gallus is an ass. He forgets he's a husband too.
    Uncle of uncles, who puts the world to bed.

78 b

At this point, I am a little sad;

to see a pure girl's lips
With pissing and kissing confounded.
You've a foul mouth;

and you won't get away with it.
The world shall hear, exactly what you are.
That old hag Gossip will tell and tell and tell.

79

Lesbius: a proper doll. Lesbia cuddles him;
Catullus is out. 'Not one of us.'
They buy and sell Catulluses -
Pour trois petites bises.

80

What's the story, Jelly-baby? How come
    Those rosebud lips so winter-white,
Morning and afternoon, when out you pop
    From bed, after a long, hard rest?
Something's up; and rumour says you suck it,
    That pouffe who makes tents in the bed.
It's obvious. Miss Victor's flashing his wares;
    Straight from the horse's mouth.

81

There's nobody in the world like him, you say,
    Dear J., no gorgeouser George to fancy
Than poppety from Pesaro (famous for its pox);
    He's bloodless as a gilded torso.
Your heart is his. You 'daresay' you prefer him to me.
    And you 'know what you're doing'. *Do* you?

82

Q., shall Catullus pledge you his eyes?
    Or what's worth more than his eyes?
Take my eyes; but don't, don't relieve me of her;
    Or take what's worth more than my eyes.

83

When her old man's about,
                Lesbia gives me non-stop hell.
The old fart thinks it 'frightfully funny'.
Ass. If our thing was off,
                Why would she say a word?
Her temperature would be normal.
Instead, bitch, bitch, bitch. *Ergo*, it's on.
More - she's in a bloody passion:
The hots! Entailing talk, talk, talk.

84

'Hadvantages,' quotha (meaning: advantages);
Ditto 'hambush' (for ambush). That's our Alf.
Boasting, boasting 'ow helegantly 'e spoke:
Hambush hambitiously hemphasised.
His mother's the same, and his uncle (Mr Freedman).
Mother's dad and his wayward wife, the same.
Official news: ALF TO MANAGE SYRIA.
Our ears relax. The Greeks? They needn't worry:
Smooth breathings will amputate his aitches.
Then horrible hintelligence harrives:
IONIAN SEA GETS ROUGH TREATMENT.
Alf's dubbed it, on landing, High-Own-Ian. What helse?

85

I hate and I love. Why do that? Good question.
No answer, save 'I do'. Nailed, through either hand.

86

QUINTIA VOTED TOPS.
                    Granted, she's a star:
Tall, blonde, good figure.
I'm not saying she hasn't her points.
They don't add up to beautiful, that's all.
Big girl, big talent, she lacks the clinching spark.
Lesbia is beautiful. The beauty of beauties.
What have the others got?
                    She's got it all.

87

No woman can say that she was loved
(And tell the truth) as Lesbia is by me.
No bond was ever struck as fast, as true,
As the love in me I found in loving you.

88

Making out, Jelly-baby?
          Making out with Mum and Sis? Mm?
Some itch! It keeps you up all night,
Bare-assed.
          And what about poor Uncle? No room
In his own bed. It stinks. It stinks
Beyond recall.
          You'll not get this one to the cleaner's:
Tethys (ancient of lays) won't touch it,
And Ocean (father of Muses) is too far gone
To wash it.
          It's the limit. The limit.
Because what can you do for an encore -
Bend double, and give yourself head?

89

'Gellius has lost a lot of weight.'
Surprise, surprise. When his mother's
So good to him and his sister's fighting fit
And sexy with it. (His uncle's v. nice to him too.)
G. never stops exercising his female relations.

Hard *not* to lose weight in the circs.
'He's never had a proper relationship.'
No, but he's got enough improper ones
To account for his being clapped out.

90

May a prophet be born, we pray,
From the *mariage sacré*
    Of Gellius and his mum.
Persian entrails shall be his reading,
For he'll have the incestuous breeding
    Whence Persian prophets come.
The child will heat dishes for the God
- Hot gravy with tripe *à la mode* -
    And a fakir's hymn he'll hum.

91

Trust you, Jelly? Why *did* I imagine I could?
I was in love, in hell, and thought you'd respect it.
Your famous honour? As found among thieves, old boy.
(Call it tabu, and your tongue's hanging out.)
No, it was because she wasn't your sister, my love,
And she wasn't your ma; hence she was safe, I thought.
I thought I knew you of old; I never guessed
That my loving her would suffice to turn you on.
It did. The sordid always sparks your appetite.
You like your game well hung. Trust you.

92

Lesbia bitch-bitch-bitches, forever knocking me.
Yet I'm damned if Lesbia loves me not.
How come? Because it's six of her and half a dozen of
  me.
I knock her constantly. And if I love her not, I'm
  damned.

93

I'm not all that interested, Caesar, whether I please you
    or not.
Who are you, anyway? Mister Black or Mister White?

94

Big Dick's a fucking pimp; a-fucking goes the pimp,
    Big Dick.
It's an old recipe: meat that makes its own gravy.

95 a

Publication day. 'Zmyrna' by Cinna, dear Cinna.
Nine harvests since he began, nine winters too.
Meanwhile, Hortensius is 500,000 lines to the good:
Tumtitty tum tum tum tumtitty tumtitty tum.
'Zmyrna' will outdo him yet. Selling everywhere!
By Satrachus' sounding stream (local boy makes good!)

And as long as ever-ageing Time can turn a page.
Volusius' Annals? Dead give-away. By Padua's bank
Soggy wrappings they'll provide, for stinking fish.

95 b

Your sweet unemphatic line means more to me
Than all Antimachus' swank, the people's choice.

96

For Calvus

There are no answers from the grave,
Yet may our grief still touch them there?
Grief that lost love brings to life again,
And friends we miss we did not miss before.
Unnecessary death must hurt Quintilia less
If she can know you love her so much, still.

97

No (so help me God), I never discriminated in any way
Between the smell of A's mouth and the smell of his arse.
In no respect was the former nicer than the latter, or
    vice versa.
I was wrong: the arse is nicer, much.
In that it comes without teeth. The mouth has teeth,
    eighteen inches long,
Like pegs stuck in a rickety cart to stop the manure
    falling out.

Another comparison: when he smiles, his grin spreads
    out
Like a cunt on a straddling mule having a steamy piss.
And this is your big man with the girls. A fucking
    charmer.
Put him on the treadmill: let him play the donkey there.
A woman who could stomach him - she's just the girl we
    want
To lick the arse of the public hangman when he's got
    the trots.

98

To you, if to anyone, Victius, you shit,
One can say what's usually said to long-winded idiots.
A tongue like yours, given the opening, could get a job
Licking arses or the toe-jam from peasants' sandals.
You wish we'd all 'jolly well disappear?'
Just open your mouth: you'll jolly well get your wish.

99

I filched a real kiss, when you were just pretending,
Juventius, my honey. Sweeter than ambrosia.
And I paid the thief's price: an hour or more
Nailed to the cross. I still have the scars.
No excuses, no mercy-pleas, no tears
Could melt by a fraction your ferocity.
You rinsed those pretty lips with gouts of water,
And wiped them clean on the back of your hand.
Yuck! The taste of my mouth on yours!
Dirty, poxy whore, piss-face: that was me.

110

That done, you handed me over to cruel Love
To be tortured with every refinement,
Not happy till that ambrosial kiss soured
To a bitter bite, sharper than hellebore.
If that's how you pay your luckless lover back,
Never again a kiss of yours I'll filch.

100

Caelius fancies Aufillenus, Quintus Aufillena:
The flower of Verona's awfully in love!
C. with the brother, Q. with the sister
(Or so they tell me: brothers in arms. *That's* nice!)
Now, whom shall I support? Caelius, you:
My only tried and trusted friend once,
When things were hot, too bloody hot, for me.
Good luck then, Caelius: go over big.

101

For this have I crossed frontiers and oceans, brother:
To sacrifice at your grim and distant tomb.
This is the last service I can render:
Empty words to wordless ashes.
Insomuch as chance has filched you from me,
My poor brother, put away without appeal,
Accept these poor and makeshift words,
Ancestral epitaph on sacrificial days.
Accept them, drenched with a brother's tears:
You are forever with me, brother, and forever gone.

102

Can I keep a secret? Are we not true friends?
As I trust you, Cornelius, and know I always can,
So do you trust me. I swear it; I'm *with* you.
Call me Harpo-crates. (Sealed lips personified.)

103

Final demand. Give back my ten sesterces.
After that, be as big a shot as you like.
Or, if you need the money, dear, stop yelling:
You can't play the pimp *and* the bigshot.

104

You think I 'might well' have written shit about her.
My love, my life. Dearer to me than both my eyes.
Well, I couldn't. (Though it 'might well' have saved
     my life, my love.)
You, you've got a mind like Tappo, prince of
     pornographers.

105 (i)

BIG DICK ATTEMPTS CLIMB MUSES' MOUNT.
They shovel him off like the shit he is.

105 (ii)

Big Dick tries to make the Muses' mount:
The Muses jerk him off, arse over tip.

106

PRETTY BOY SEEN WITH AUCTIONEER.
Rumour says, going, going, gone.

107

You long and long for something,
Knowing it's hopeless. And it happens.
That is pleasure indeed. Lesbia
Is mine, and I have that pleasure.
Forget gold. You're back
And I had given up hope.
Your idea, what's more. The sun's full out.
I must be the luckiest man alive.
What else could one want from life?

108

For Cominius. By popular decision.

Suppose your venerable old age were to be
Terminated on grounds of moral turpitude.
I've a strong feeling that your tongue might be ripped out
(No one likes it) and given to a peckish vulture.
A black-throated crow could enjoy your dug-out eyes,
Your tripe the dogs, and wolves could lick the plates.

109

We shall never quarrel again, you say,
But love and love forever, you and I.
Dear God, may the promise hold,
Let her really mean what she says.
We *must* live our whole lives together,
Sealed in the quintessential bond.

110

To Aufillena

Girls who play it straight never lack admirers:
They name their price and begin as they mean to go on.
You say you will and then you won't, you bitch;
You can take, but you won't give. You do the dirt.

Be grown up and fuck or be a child and don't,
But you can't have a box-office and not give a show.
That's worse than your thoroughgoing tart,
Who at least goes the whole hog in her whoring.

111

Aufillena again

'She was glad never to know any man but her husband':
The praise of praises for a wife.
But you might as well open your legs to the lot
As produce more cousins by having your uncle's kids.

112

You're a big man, Naso, and it takes a bigger man
To fuck you: you're a big man, and a bigger bum.

113

When Pompey was first consul, Cinna, two men
Frequented the First Lady. Now he's consul again
The same two are at it again - with a thousand more
Up to the same. Fucking inflation again.

114

They tell me that Big Dick's struck it rich at Firmum:
Huntin', shootin', fishin': the jackpot, no less.
No good, though: he still can't balance his books.
So let him play the squire - rich Mr Nobody.
He'd look the part, if he didn't have egg on his face.

115

Big Dick's gone to ground: he's the proud owner
Of thirty acres of farmland, forty of pasture -
And a dirty great bog besides. O Croesus,
That one man alone should own so much:
Field, meadow, mighty forest, bog and marsh
Horizon to horizon, everywhere you look!
Big, big stuff; and he's the biggest stuff of all:
The cock of the walk, the walking cock.

116

In anxious, constant search I racked my brains
        For poems of Callimachus to send
You, Gellius - to please by taking pains,
        And bring your short, sharp missives to an end.
A waste of time (I see that now): my pleas
        Were useless. Fine! Sharp-shoot away: your aim
Is poor, I pirouette aside with ease.
        And *I* shoot bull's-eyes, sure to kill, or maim.

Index of first lines

117

118

120